MACHINE LEARNING

WITH PYTHON

*Advanced Guide in Machine Learning
with Python*

PAIGE JACOBS

TABLE OF CONTENTS

Introduction

In the course of advancing digitalization in almost all areas of life, machine learning and artificial intelligence play an important strategic role in the economic, civil, and military fields.

As a result, they are increasingly becoming the focus of politics, science, and industry to compete globally for research and development successes, talents, data, and commercial applications.

In the USA, too, worried voices are expressing themselves in AI- and ML-based Research and Technology, in particular from China, but to be overtaken by Russia.

I have designed this guide to give you an overview of the advanced Machine Learning activities with a particular focus on Python as an excellent programing language.

We can understand the subject of machine learning via different approaches. We will start with its conceptualization and its main applications.

The use of practice-oriented code examples serves a crucial purpose; concrete examples clarify the general concepts by putting what has been learned into practice immediately. However, one must not forget that great responsibility always accompanies great power.

In addition to the direct experience of putting machine learning into practice using the Python programming language and Python-based learning libraries, this book also presents the mathematical concepts underlying the machine learning algorithms that are indispensable for the successful use of machine learning.

So this book is not a purely practical work, but a book that discusses the necessary details of the concepts of advanced machine learning with Python, explains how learning algorithms work and how to use them in an understandable, yet informative way, and - more importantly - shows how to avoid the most common mistakes.

If you enter the search term, machine learning, on Google Scholar, you will get a considerable number (about 4,760,000) of hits as a result. Of course, in this book, we can't discuss all the details of the algorithms and applications developed over the last 60 years.

However, we will embark on an exciting tour that covers all the crucial topics and concepts needed for you to get a thorough introduction. If your thirst for knowledge is not satisfied, even after reading, there are a variety of other resources available that you can use to track the critical advances in the field.

If you already have some background in machine learning and know the basics, you can use this book, the third, in a series, to put your knowledge into practice. If you have already used such techniques, but would like to understand better how they work, you will also get your money's worth here.

And if you're new to machine learning, you've got all the more reason to be happy, because I can promise you that this process will change the way you think about your future tasks - and I want to show you how you can tackle problems by unleashing the power inherent in the data.

Before we go into machine learning in more detail, we would like to answer a question you are likely asking right now - Why Python? The answer is quite simple – it is the most powerful programming language, yet incredibly easy to learn. Python is the most popular programming language in the field of data science because it eliminates the hassle of programming and provides an environment in which you can implement your ideas and concepts immediately.

We, the authors, can say from our own experience that, by working with machine learning, we have become better scientists, thinkers, and problem solvers. In this book, we would like to share our insights with you. We acquire knowledge through learning, which in turn requires a particular zeal, and only practice makes the proverbial master.

The road ahead won't always be easy, and some of the issues are much more difficult than others, but we hope that you take the opportunity and concentrate on the reward of your effort. As the book progresses, you will be able to add several powerful techniques to your repertoire that will help you master even the most difficult tasks in a data-driven manner.

What will you explore through the journey to this book?

Chapter 1: How Computers Can Learn From Data introduces you to the most important parts of machine learning, used to tackle various problems. We also discuss the necessary steps in designing a typical machine learning model, which we refer to in the following chapters.

Chapter 2: Installing Python Anaconda for the Machine Learning Algorithms for Classification, goes back to the beginnings of machine learning, and introduces the proper installation process. This chapter cautiously includes the ML Algorithms & Colab classification and focuses on the interaction of optimization algorithms and machine learning.

Chapter 3: Predicting Continuous Target Variables of Logistic Regression with Python by Regression Analysis, discusses advanced procedures for modeling linear relationships between target variables and regressors to predict continuous values.

Chapter 4: K-Means Data Grouping: Learn Your Concepts, Definitions, and Applications I went through all phases of the K-Means algorithm. And the definition of grouping. You will understand how the whole grouping process works, its benefits, and challenges. In this chapter, you will also see in practice how to apply the concepts learned by running the K-means algorithm and analyzing the results step by step.

Chapter 5: The purpose of this post is to explain what decision trees are, what they are for, how to build one from data, among other things. I won't go in-depth in detail on some subjects. We will deal with some relatively complicated concepts like information gain and entropy, but this will not prevent us from having a stable version of the algorithm.

Chapter 6: Predicting Continuous Target Variables by Linear Regression Analysis, discusses advanced procedures for modeling linear relationships between target variables and regressors to predict continuous values.

Chapter 7: Implementation of an Artificial Neural Network, extends the concept of gradient-based optimization introduced in Chapter 2 to create robust, multi-layer neural networks based on the conventional backpropagation algorithm.

Chapter 8: Modeling sequential data using recurrent neural networks, introduces another typical neural network architecture for deep learning that is particularly well suited for processing sequential data and time series. In this chapter, we will apply various recurrent neural network architectures to text data. As a warm-up exercise, we first consider a mood analysis and then create entirely new texts.

Chapter 9: In this final chapter, we will familiarize you with the most common clustering methods, the K -nearest algorithm, its application libraries, classes, k-Nearest Neighbor with Scikit - Learn, and modules necessary for the execution of the algorithm k -means in python.

CHAPTER
ONE

How Computers Can Learn From Data

Experts understand machine learning as a key technology of artificial intelligence, which, in turn, is a computer science branch designed to enable machines to perform tasks "intelligently." Neither "intelligent" nor the techniques used are defined. The first commercially significant successes in the field of AI were achieved with so-called expert systems with a manually constructed knowledge base.

With such manual knowledge inputs or even the explicit programming of a solution, however, one has failed with more complex AI tasks. An alternative to this is machine learning, which today represents the critical technology of intelligent systems.

Machine learning aims at the generation of "Knowledge" from "experience," in which learning algorithms from examples develop a complex model. The model, and thus the automatically acquired knowledge representation, can then be applied to new, potentially unknown data of the same type.

Whenever processes are too complicated to be described analytically, but a sufficient amount of sample data - such as sensor data, images, or texts - is available, machine learning is the answer. With the models learned, predictions can be made, or recommendations and decisions can be generated - without any rules or calculation rules defined in advance.

ML applications or "learning machines" are not only limited to physical devices and robots but can also be purely digital applications in IT systems, such as various types of "robots" and bots, for example, chatbots, social bots, game bots or robo players, Robo advisors or robot journalists. ML-techniques and AI-applications are in the process of sustaining all industries and areas of life to influence the way we do things. There is enormous global competition for this future field, which is being fought between the USA and China in particular.

However, the often astonishing performances of ML- and AI-based systems do not imply that the machine has any understanding or even awareness of what data it is processing, why, and in what context it is processing.

And what the meaning of the data is. Even a human-like "artificial universal intelligence" or even an "artificial super-intelligence," as it is often portrayed in the media and propagated by some researchers and industry representatives, will realistically play no role in the foreseeable future. However, the scenarios discussed draw attention to any general risks.

The existing ML applications are designed with a great effort and are only trained and ready for use for small tasks. Current research is primarily concerned with reducing the training effort, improving the robustness, security, and transparency of the models, making them easier to adapt to new tasks, and to combine the competencies of man and machine purposefully.

A Brief Historical Overview

Machine learning can look back on quite a long history and has emerged from methods of statistics and AI. Stimulated by the understanding of distributed neuronal processes in the brain, the first concepts of artificial neuronal networks (KNN) were developed in the late 1940s and implemented ten years later.

At the end of the 1960s, two well-known AI scientists, Minsky and Papert, showed that even a single neuron could not learn the elementary logic of either-or logic and that larger neuronal networks with few local networks were limited in their expressiveness. That led to the staging of AI research in the 1970s, especially at KNN, and introduced the so-called first "AI winter."

In the 1980s, research concentrated on symbolic expert systems. Their knowledge base consisted of manually entered logical rules that related to manually selected characteristics or manually constructed object hierarchies. Such representations of knowledge are called "symbolic knowledge." It turned out, however, that a consistent expansion of more extensive knowledge bases became more and more difficult. It was recognized that practically all conceivable preconditions for action could never be explicitly specified. Also, problems arose in dealing with new information that contradicted what had already been entered. That led to the second "AI winter."

In the mid-1980s, neural networks became interesting again through the back-propagation method. For practical applications, however, learning methods such as support vector machines turned out to be more manageable from 1995 onwards.

It was the turn of the millennium before advances in computer technologies, and the emergence of "big data" made it possible to learn very complex, so-called "deep" artificial neural networks. That was the beginning of the success of today's AI.

Learning Tasks, Learning Styles, Models, And Algorithms

In machine learning, a distinction is made between learning styles that are suitable for different purposes. Depending on which additional information is available, other tasks can be learned. In supervised learning, the correct answers must be given to the following examples, supplied as so-called labels. The specification of labels usually means more work for data preprocessing, but is necessary if objects are to be classified and values estimated or predicted.

In unsupervised learning, on the other hand, the raw example data is sufficient to discover basic patterns in the data. In empowering learning, machines use feedback from their interaction with the environment to future actions and reduce errors. This type of learning is often used in robotics, for example, to learn the best gripping movements for objects.

There are now a large number of model types and learning procedures or concrete learning algorithms that are particularly suitable for different tasks. The most common ones are listed in the following table.

Kaggle, a platform for ML competitions, asked in 2017 in a survey about the methods used. Figure 1 shows the result based on 7 301 responses. Ensemble methods and "gradient boosted machines" combine several models, mostly decision trees, for classification and regression tasks. CNN and RNN belong to the deep neural networks.

Learning Style	Learning Task	Learning Methods	Model
Monitored	regression	Linear Regression	regression line
		Classification and regression tree procedure (CART)	regression tree
	classification	Logistic Regression	dividing line
		Iterative Dichotomizer (ID3)	decision tree
		Support Vector Machine (SVM)	hyperplane
		Bayesian inference	Bayesian models

Unsupervised	clustering	K-Means	cluster centers
	dimension reduction	Kernel Principal Component Analysis (PCA)	Composite characteristics
Encouraging	Sequential decision making	Q-Learning	strategies
Various	Various	backward propagation	Artificial neural networks

Common Learning Methods and their Models

Deep Neural Networks

Since 2006, deep learning or learning with deep artificial neural networks has made enormous progress, especially in the analysis of images, video, speech, and text data. Meanwhile, machines with deep KNN can, in some cases, identify faces and objects with a lower error rate than humans and even professionals4.

Also, such machines can solve novel learning tasks with complex results such as translating texts, answering questions and e-mails, sending and receiving messages, etc. to reports, compose music and texts or produce pictures.

The deep KNN consist of many layers of "nodes" realized in software, characterized as artificial neurons (see Fig. 2). When learning, the weights, which are numerical values at the connections between the nodes, are changed until the outputs are good enough.

In their inner layers, the networks independently extract compact representations from the raw data, which makes many pre-processing programs redundant and makes the actual task easier to learn. Deep KNN form expressive models that can also be trained in parallel computer systems.

That often works but is only useful with vast amounts of data. Since it is not easy for people to understand what the weightings in a CNN mean and how exactly the expenses are incurred, we speak here of "sub-symbolic" models, in contrast to symbolic models such as the decision trees (see Fig. 3) or the knowledge bases of earlier expert systems.

There is a multitude of network architectures that have proven to be useful for different data types and tasks. Since the networks as a whole can be trained from the raw data to the output, this is also referred to as end-to-end learning. A very successful application of deep KNN is the "Deep Q-Networks" in encouraging end-to-end learning5 for games and robots.

Solving Interactive Tasks through Enhanced Learning

The third variant of machine learning is reinforcement learning. Here the objective is to develop a system (the *agent*) that improves its performance through interactions with its *environment.*

Information about the current state of the environment typically includes a so-called *reward signal*, so reinforcement learning is, to some extent, related to *supervised learning.*

However, this feedback is not the correct class name or value, but a measure of how good the action was, described by a *reward function.*

The agent can recognize which actions are particularly well rewarded by interactions with his environment through strengthening learning. This can be done by simple trial and error or by conscious planning.

An excellent example of reinforcement learning is a chess computer. Here the agent evaluates the position on the chessboard (the surroundings) after a series of moves, and the reward can be defined at the end of the game as *victory* or *defeat.*

There are a variety of different subspecies of reinforcement learning. In general, however, in reinforcement learning, the agent tries to maximize the reward through a series of interactions with the environment.

Each state can be assigned a positive (or negative) rating, and the reward can be defined by achieving an overall goal, such as winning or losing a chess game. In chess, for example, the result of each move can be interpreted as a different state of the environment.

To stay with chess: Imagine reaching certain positions on the chessboard as a positive event - for example, hitting an opponent's piece or threatening the queen.

Other positions are negative if, for example, one of the player's moves can be beaten on the next move. Of course, not every move leads to the capture of a character, so reinforcement learning tries to learn a series of steps by maximizing a reward based on immediate or delayed feedback.

While this section provides a basic overview of reinforcement learning, the topic goes beyond the scope of this book, which focuses on classification, regression analysis, and clustering.

Identify Hidden Structures through Unsupervised Learning

In supervised learning, the correct answer is known in advance when training the model, and in reinforcement learning, we define an evaluation or *reward* for specific actions of the agent. In unsupervised learning, on the other hand, we are dealing with unmarked data or data of *unknown structure*.

Through the procedures used in unsupervised learning, we can explore the structure of the data to extract meaningful information from it without any indication of a target variable or reward function.

Tracking Subgroups through Clustering

Clustering is an explorative data analysis method that allows us to divide information into meaningful subgroups (*clusters*) without prior knowledge of the group affiliation of this information. Each cluster that occurs during the analysis defines a group of objects that have specific properties in common but are sufficiently different from objects in other groups.

That is why clustering is sometimes referred to as "unsupervised classification." It is excellent for structuring information and deriving meaningful relationships between data. For example, it allows marketing professionals to group customers according to their interests to develop targeted campaigns.

The following figure illustrates how the clustering process can be used to organize unmarked data into three different groups, each with similar characteristics to $x1$ and $x2$.

Data Compression through Dimension Reduction

Dimensional reduction is another sub-discipline of unsupervised learning. We often have to deal with data of high dimensionality (each observation consists of a multitude of measured values), which can pose a challenge due to the limitations of storage space and computing power applied to the learning algorithms.

When pre-processing features, an unsupervised dimensional reduction is often used to free the data from so-called "noise." However, this can lead to a weakening of the significance of specific prediction algorithms. The data is divided into smaller subspaces of lesser dimensionality, with most of the relevant information retained.

In some cases, dimension reduction is also useful for visualizing the data. For example, high-dimensional feature sets can be projected onto one-, two- or three-dimensional feature spaces to display them as 3-D or 2-D scatter diagrams or histograms. The figure shows an example in which a nonlinear dimensional reduction was applied to a 3-D point set in the form of a biscuit roll to transform it into a two-dimensional feature space.

Basic Terminology And Notation

Now that we have discussed the three types of machine learning supervised, unsupervised, and reinforcement learning - we will next clarify the basic terms used in the following chapters.

The illustration shows an excerpt of the *iris data collection*, a classic example for the field of machine learning. These are measured data from 150 irises of three different species: *Iris setosa, Iris versicolor,* and *Iris virginica.*

Each of the floral specimens is represented in this data collection by a line is represented. The individual columns contain the measurement data given in centimeters, which we also refer to as *characteristics of* the amount of data.

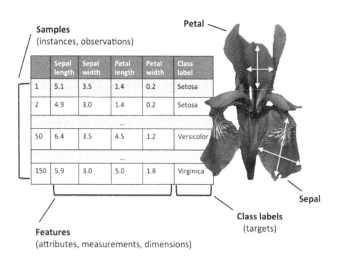

Samples
(instances, observations)

	Sepal length	Sepal width	Petal length	Petal width	Class label
1	5.1	3.5	1.4	0.2	Setosa
2	4.9	3.0	1.4	0.2	Setosa
			...		
50	6.4	3.5	4.5	1.2	Versicolor
			...		
150	5.9	3.0	5.0	1.8	Virginica

Petal

Sepal

Class labels
(targets)

Features
(attributes, measurements, dimensions)

To keep notation and implementation efficient but straightforward, we use the basics of *linear algebra*. In the following chapters, we will use matrix and vector notation to describe the data. We follow the usual convention that a row represents each object in the matrix *X,* and each character is stored as a separate column.

The iris data collection consists of 150 data sets with four characteristics each and can, therefore, be written as $X \in \mathbb{R}^{150 \times 4}$ as a 150×4 matrix:

$$\begin{bmatrix} x_1^{(1)} & x_2^{(1)} & x_3^{(1)} & x_4^{(1)} \\ x_1^{(2)} & x_2^{(2)} & x_3^{(2)} & x_4^{(2)} \\ \vdots & \vdots & \vdots & \vdots \\ x_1^{(150)} & x_2^{(150)} & x_3^{(150)} & x_4^{(150)} \end{bmatrix}$$

From now on, we will use a superscript i and a subscript j to refer to the *i-th* training object or the *j-th* dimension of the training data set.

We note vectors in $\left(x \in \mathbb{R}^{n \times 1}\right)$ bold lower case and matrices $(X \in \mathbb{R}^{n \times m})$ in bold upper case. We use italic letters to refer to single elements of a vector or a matrix ($x^{(n)}$ or $x_{(m)}^{(n)}$).

For example, the x_1^{150} first dimension of the flower copy 150 is the length of the sepal. Each row of the characteristic matrix represents a specimen of a blood and can be written   as a four-dimensional row vector, e.g.:

$$x^{(i)} = \begin{bmatrix} x_1^{(i)} & x_2^{(i)} & x_3^{(i)} & x_4^{(i)} \end{bmatrix}$$

Each characteristic dimension is a 150-dimensional column vector $x_j \in \mathbb{R}^{150 \times 1}$:

$$x_j = \begin{bmatrix} x_j^{(1)} \\ x_j^{(2)} \\ \vdots \\ x_j^{(150)} \end{bmatrix}$$

The target variables (here the class names) are also noted as 150-dimensional column vectors:

$$y = \begin{bmatrix} y^{(1)} \\ \ldots \\ y^{(150)} \end{bmatrix} \left(y \in \{\text{Setosa, Versicolor, Virginica}\} \right)$$

Development of a System for Machine Learning

In the previous sections, we have discussed the basic concepts of machine learning and the three different ways of learning. In this section, we deal with further vital components of a system for this procedure, which accompanies the learning algorithm.

The following diagram shows the typical process used in machine learning in *predictive models*, which we will look at in the following sections.

Machine Learning with Python

Python is one of the most popular programming languages in the field of data science, so there are many useful libraries developed by the Python community.

The performance of interpreted languages such as Python is inferior to that of compiled programming languages, but there are extension libraries such as *NumPy* and *SciPy that are* based on machine-oriented Fortran and C implementations to perform fast calculations with multidimensional arrays.

For machine learning tasks, we will mostly use *Scikit- learn*, a widely used and easily understandable open-source library for machine learning.

Challenges of Machine Learning

Machine learning as a data-supported technology presents quite different challenges than classical programming. As a general rule, the more training data a learning algorithm receives, the better it can improve its model and reduce the error rate. The trick is to keep the model general enough so that it can be used for new data that is not available in the training phase worked well. Also, the models should be robust, i.e., they should react similarly to similar inputs.

The quality of a model also depends on the quality of the training data. If the algorithm is shown too many wrong examples, it cannot learn the correct answers. If the examples are not representative, the expenditure on new types of input is also subject to more significant uncertainty. However, some models can also provide an assessment of how sound the output is together with their output.

A desirable and vital characteristic is the traceability of the models in general and their results in individual cases. Decision trees are particularly easy to interpret, whereas deep neural networks are poor.

The excellent scalability with increasing data volumes, on the one hand, and the poor traceability, on the other hand, are the reasons why the experts consulted in the project deep learning for necessary but not sufficient for successful ML applications.

The choice of method should always depend on the requirements of the task. We hope there will continue to be many areas of application for classical learning methods in the future that require less data - such as the support vector machines and core methods that are represented here. However, experts see even more significant potential in the combination of machine learning methods with other forms of knowledge.

Summary of the Chapter

In this chapter, we have taken a very general look at the topic of Machine Learning and familiarized ourselves with the overall picture as well as the basic concepts that we will look at in more detail in the following chapters. We have learned that supervised learning consists of two main areas: classification and regression. Classification models make it possible to assign objects to known classes, and we can use regression analysis to predict the continuous values of a target variable.

Unsupervised learning not only provides practical methods for finding structures in unmarked data, but it can also be used in pre-processing for data compression. We have briefly looked at the typical procedure for applying machine learning to problems, which serves as a basis for further discussion and practical examples in the following chapters. Also, we have set up our Python environment and updated the required packages and are now ready to watch Machine Learning in action.

In the remainder of the book, we will introduce machine learning and various methods for preprocessing data, which help to achieve the best performance with different learning algorithms. We will look at classification algorithms in quite a detail throughout the book, but also at some regression analysis and clustering techniques.

We have an exciting tour ahead of us on which many powerful methods from the broad field of machine learning will be discussed. However, we proceed step by step and build on the knowledge gradually acquired in the individual chapters.

CHAPTER

TWO

Install Anaconda Python Development Environment for Machine Learning, ML Algorithms & Colab

To program your own Artificial Intelligence Machine, you will need to have your local development environment ready on your desktop or laptop computer. In this very first chapter, we will explain a simple way to configure Python and the libraries needed to program as a Data Scientist and use the most popular Machine Learning algorithms.

Main Algorithms used in Machine Learning

In this stage of study on Machine Learning, I have encountered several algorithms that I am reusing for problem-solving and that are repeated more frequently. I will make a list with a brief description of the main algorithms used in Machine Learning. Also, each one will have links to Python code development examples.

Let us begin!

Regression Algorithms

Regression algorithms model the relationship between different variables (features) using an error measure that will be tried to minimize in an iterative process to be able to make predictions "as accurate as possible." They are widely used in statistical analysis. The classic example is the prediction of Real Estate prices based on their characteristics: number of floor environments, neighborhood, distance to the center, square meters of the floor, etc.

The most used Regression Algorithms are:

- Linear Regression

- Logistic Regression

Instance-Based Algorithms

They are Learning Models for decision problems with instances or examples (samples) of training data that are important or required by the model.

They are also called Algorithms «Winner takes everything» and memory-based learning in which a model is created from a database, and new data is added comparing its similarity with existing samples to find «the best match »And make the prediction.

The most used instance-based algorithms are:

- k-Nearest Neighbor (kNN)

- Self-Organizing Map

Decision Tree Algorithms

They model the decision making based on the current (real) values of the attributes that our data have. They are used primarily for classification of information, forking, and modeling the possible paths are taken and their probability of occurrence to improve their accuracy. Once armed, the decision trees run very fast to get results.

The most used decision tree algorithms are:

- Classification and Regression Trees (CART)
- Conditional Tree Decision
- Random Forest

Bayesian Algorithms

They are algorithms that explicitly use the Bayes Probability Theorem for Classification and Regression problems.

The most used are:

- Naive Bayes
- Gaussian Naive Bayes
- Multinomial Naive Bayes
- Bayesian Network

Clustering Algorithms (grouping)

They are used to group existing data that we do not know about their characteristics in common or want to discover.

These methods attempt to create "central points" and hierarchies to differentiate groups and discover common characteristics by proximity.

The most used are:

- K-Means

- K-Medians

- Hierarchical Clustering

Neural Network Algorithms

They are algorithms and structures inspired by the biological functions of neural networks.

They are often used for classification and regression problems, but they have great potential to solve many problems. They are very good at detecting patterns. Artificial Neural Networks required a lot of processing and memory capacity and were very limited by the technology of the past until these last years in which they resurfaced with great force giving rise to Deep Learning (detailed below).

The basic and classic neural networks are:

- XOR Gate

- Perceptron

- Back-Propagation

- Hopfield Network

- MLP: Multi-Layered Perceptron

Deep Learning Algorithms

They are the evolution of the Artificial Neural Networks that take advantage of the cheaper technology and the higher capacity for execution, memory, and disk to exploit a large amount of data in substantial neural networks interconnect them in various layers that can be executed in parallel to perform calculations.

The most popular Deep Learning algorithms are:

- Convolutional Neural Networks

- Long Short Term Memory Neural Networks

Dimension Reduction Algorithms

They seek to exploit the existing structure in an unsupervised manner to simplify the data and reduce or compress it.

They are useful for visualizing data or for simplifying the set of variables that a supervised algorithm can then use.

The most used are:

- Principal Component Analysis (PCA)

- t-SNE

Natural Language Processing (NLP)

Natural Language Processing is a mix between DataScience, Machine Learning, and Linguistics. It aims to understand human language. In both texts and speech/voice. From analyzing syntactically or grammatically thousands of contents, automatically classifying topics, chatbots, and even generating poetry imitating Shakespeare.

It is also common to use it for the Analysis of Feelings in social networks (for example, concerning a politician) and automatic translation between languages. It can even be used for voice assistants like Siri, Cortana, and the possibility of asking and getting answers or even getting movie tickets.

Other Algorithms

- Learning Algorithms by Association Rules

- Set Algorithms

- Computer Vision

- Recommendation Systems

Remember that all these algorithms are vulnerable to problems of Underfitting and Overfitting that we must take into account and solve.

Why Install Python and Anaconda on my Computer?

Python is a simple, fast and light language and is ideal for learning, experimenting, practicing and working with machine learning, neural networks and deep learning - among others -.

We will use the Anaconda Suite that will facilitate the task of installing the environment and will include the Jupyter Notebooks, which is an application that will help us do step-by-step exercises in Machine Learning, creates data visualizations and writes comments as if they were a notebook of college or university.

This Suite is cross-platform and can be used for Windows, Linux, and Macintosh. In my case, I will download the version for my MacBook Pro, but for another operating system, it will be similar.

Agenda of the Future Data Scientist

Our agenda list includes:

1. Download Anaconda

2. Install Anaconda

3. Start and Update Anaconda

4. Update Scikit-learn package

5. Install Libraries for Deep Learning

Let's start!

1. Download Anaconda

In step one, we will see how to download anaconda to our disk and obtain this scientific Python suite.

We headed to the Home of Anaconda and went to the section Download (downloads)

We choose our platform: Windows, Mac or Linux (in my case I will select Apple's)

Attention: Choose the Python 3.6 version (and not the 2.7 version) and select the Graphical Installer.

With this, we will save on our hard disk about 620MB (according to the operating system), and we will obtain a file with the name similar to Anaconda3-5.1.10-MacOSX-x86_64.pkg.

2. Install Anaconda

In step two, we will install the app on our system. (You must have Administrator permissions if you install for all users).

We execute the file we download by double-clicking.

A "Typical Wizard" installation will open.

We will follow the steps; we can select installation only for our user, select the disk path where we will install and ready.

When installing the total size, you can exceed 1GB on disk.

3. Start and Update Anaconda

In this step, we will verify that it has been installed correctly and verify to have the most recent version.

Anaconda comes with a suite of graphic tools called «Anaconda Navigator.» Let's start the application, and we will see a screen like this:

Among others, we see that we can launch the Jupyter Notebooks! (I will write specifically about this later).

To verify the installation, we open a Mac / Linux / Ubuntu Terminal or the Windows Command-Line.

We wrote

1   conda -V

and we get the version

1   conda 4.3.30

then we type

1   python -V

and verify the Python version of our system.

To make sure we have the most recent version of the suite, we will run

1   conda update conda

we must put 'and' to update and they will be downloaded. Then we execute

1   conda update anaconda

To confirm that everything works fine, we will create a text file to write a short python script. Name the file versions.py and its content will be:

```
1     # scipy
2     import scipy
3     print('scipy: %s' % scipy.__version__)
4     # numpy
5     import numpy
6     print('numpy: %s' % numpy.__version__)
7     # matplotlib
8     import matplotlib
9     print('matplotlib: %s' % matplotlib.__version__)
10    # pandas
11    import pandas
```

```
12      print('pandas: %s' % pandas.__version__)
13      # statsmodels
14      import statsmodels
15      print('statsmodels: %s' % statsmodels.__version__)
16      # scikit-learn
17      import sklearn
18      print('sklearn: %s' % sklearn.__version__)
```

In the command line, in the same directory where the file is, we will write:

```
1       python versiones.py
```

and we should see an output similar to this:

```
1       scipy: 0.18.1
2       numpy: 1.12.1
3       matplotlib: 1.5.3
4       pandas: 0.19.2
5       statsmodels: 0.8.0
6       sklearn: 0.18.1
```

4. Update scikit-learn library

In this step, we will update the most used library for Machine Learning in python called SciKit Learn

In the Terminal we will write

1   conda update scikit-learn

We must confirm the update by putting 'y' in the terminal.

We can re-verify that everything is correct by executing

1   python versiones.py

5. Install libraries for Deep Learning

In this step, we will install the libraries used for Deep Learning. Specifically, they will be keras - new tutorial Simple Neural Network - the famous and beloved Google Tensorflow.

To do this, we will execute on our command line

1   conda install -c conda-forge tensorflow

1   pip install keras

And we will create a new script to prove that they were installed correctly. We will call versions_deep.py, and it will have the following lines:

1   # tensorflow

2   import tensorflow

3   print('tensorflow: %s' % tensorflow.__version__)

4   # keras

5   import keras

6   print('keras: %s' % keras.__version__)

We execute in the command line

```
1        python versiones_deep.py
```

In the terminal and we will see the exit:

```
1        tensorflow: 1.0.1

2        Using TensorFlow backend.

3        keras: 2.0.2
```

We already have our development environment prepared for combat. For our Machine Learning career, the confrontation with Big Data, and the improvement as a Data Scientist, we need a good environment in which to program and "slap" -lease, try things and have fun. For this, we have the Anaconda free tools suite that offers a friendly and simple environment in which to create our machines in Python code.

Machine Learning in the Cloud: Google Collaboratory with GPU!

Incredible as it may seem, right now, we have a free account available to program our Machine Learning models in the cloud, with Python, Jupyter Notebooks remotely, and even with GPU to increase our processing power ... free! Yes, yes, this is not an "uncle's story," nor does it have any trap! ... Discover how to take advantage of it in this section!

Machine Learning from the Browser

First thing's first. Why will I want to have my code in the cloud? Well, the standard (ideal?) is that we have a local development environment on our computer, a test environment on some server, staging, and production. But what if we do not have the environment installed yet?

Or we have conflicts with a file/library, Python version, or for whatever reason we do not have disk space or even if it is very slow and we do not have a higher processor/ram? Or even for simple convenience, it is always good to have an online website, "always ready," where almost all the software we need is installed.

And that service is provided by Google, among other options. The exciting thing is that Google Colab It offers several advantages over its competitors.

Interestingly, Google Colab offers several advantages over its competitors.

The GPU... At Home or in the Cloud

A GPU? Why do I want that if I already have about 8 cores? The reality is that for the processing of machine learning algorithms (and for video games, ahem!) The GPU is much more powerful in performing calculations (also in parallel), for example, matrix multiplications ... those that WE DO ALL the time to TRAIN our models !!!

To make the descent by gradient or Toooodo time with the Backpropagation of our neural networks, this is an improvement of up to 10x in processing speed. Algorithms that used to take days are now resolved in hours — a huge breakthrough.

If you have a Nvidia card with GPU already installed, congratulations, you already have the power! If you do not have it and you are not going to invest a few dollars to buy it, you can have all (*) its power from the cloud!

(*) **NOTE:** Google reserves the right to limit the use of GPU if it considers that you are abusing or using that resource too much or for improper purposes (e.g., bitcoin mining).

What is Google Colab?

Google Colab is a cloud service, which provides us with a Jupyter Notebook that we can access with a web browser regardless of whether "at home" we use Windows, Linux, or Mac. It has great advantages:

- Possibility to activate a GPU

- We can share the code easily

- It is based on Jupyter notebook, and we will find a familiar environment

- We can create books in Python 2 or 3

- It has preinstalled the standard libraries used in data science and the possibility of installing others that we need

- By linking to our Google Drive account, we can read from their input CSV files or save output images, etc.

How is GoogleColab Used?

First of all, we enter and log in with our Google account in Collaboratory. Now we can:

- Create a new notebook:

  o Let's «File -> create a new notebook in Python 3»

- and enable GPU:

  o We go to «Execution Environment -> Change type of execution environment» and choose «Hardware Accelerator» GPU

Link to Google Drive

An advantage of linking our account with Drive is because it makes it easier for us to upload or download files. To upload a file, select "Files" from the left panel and click on the "upload" button.

But if you want to be able to use any file, for example. csv that you have in your drive unit, you must run in a cell:

1 from google.colab import drive

2 drive.mount('/content/drive/')

It will ask you to click on a link and write a code that will give you when you authorize the app. When you come back and update the file tab, you will see your unit mounted and ready to use!

Run a Github Jupyter Notebook

We are going to open a Jupyter Notebook and do this in the "Open notebook" box.

1. We select GITHUB,

2. We copy the repository address, in our case https://github.com/jbagnato/machine-learning/

3. and we give the magnifying glass to search.

4. The list with the repo files will appear.

5. And from there we select the notebook called Exercise_CNN.ipynb

We will see that we have the same Notebook but in Google Colab

Download a Resource to the Notebook

ALMOST EVERYTHING… but we still have something left before we can execute. In this exercise, we need to have 70,000 images in their respective directories.

To do this, we will first download the ZIP. We create a new cell and execute, for example:

we get https://github.com/abcd/machine-learning/raw/master/sportimages.zip

and we will see that our zip file appears in the list (click on «Update» if necessary).

Unzip a File in the Notebook

And now we must decompress it, create a cell, and execute:

! unzip -uq 'sportimages.zip' -d '.'

REMEMBER to enable the GPU runtime environment as we saw before. Now we can run all the cells and see how fast the CNN runs with GPU, compared to CPU. It takes from 4 minutes to only 40 seconds.

Install other Python Libraries with Pip

We must execute, for example:! Pip install gensim

We have seen that we have the option of having our local development environment but also this alternative of being able to program, experiment, and work in the cloud. Thanks to this service, we can have the environment ready in a few seconds and take advantage of the advantages it offers us, especially the use of GPU, which is a resource that not everyone has. I hope you enjoyed the colab section as well as the entire chapter.

CHAPTER
THREE

Logistic Regression with Python

Brief Introduction to Logistic Regression

We will use Machine Learning algorithms in Python to solve a Logistic Regression problem. From a set of input data (characteristics), our output will be discrete (and not continuous), so we use Logistic Regression (and not Linear Regression). Logistic Regression is a Supervised Algorithm and is used for classification.

We are going to classify problems with two possible "YES / NO" states: binary or a finite number of "tags" or "classes": multiple. Some Examples of Logistic Regression are:

- Sort if the mail that arrives is Spam or Not Spam

- Given the clinical results of a tumor, classified as "Benign" or "Malignant."

- The text of an article to analyze is: Entertainment, Sports, Politics or Science

- From the bank history, grant credit or not

We will rely on the implementation of the sklearn package in Python to put it into practice.

Logistic Regression Exercise in Python

For our project, I have created a CSV file with input data as an example to classify if the user who visits a website uses Windows, Macintosh, or Linux operating system.

Our input information is 4 features that I took from a website that uses Google Analytics and are:

- Duration of the visit in Seconds

- Number of Pages Viewed during the Session

- Number of User Actions (click, scroll, use of checkbox, sliders, etc.)

- Sum of the Value of the shares (each share has a critical assessment associated)

Since the output is discrete, we will assign the following values to the tags:

0 - Windows

1 - Macintosh

2 - Linux

The sample is small: there are 170 records to understand the project but remember that to achieve good results, it is always better to have an abundant number of data that will give greater accuracy to the predictions and avoid problems of overfitting or underfitting. (To say something, from one thousand to 5,000 records would not be bad).

Technical Requirements

To run the code, you need to have Python installed - both version 2.7 or 3.6 - and several packages commonly used in Data Science. I recommend having the Anaconda or Canopy suite installed, very simple, and with the "Data Science" packages already pre-installed, and they work on all platforms.

For this example, we will create a Jupyter block of notes below where the exercise is shown step by step.

Logistic Regression with SKLearn:

Identify User Operating System

To start, we make the necessary Import with the packages that we will use in the Exercise.

```
1      import pandas as pd

2      import numpy as np

3      from sklearn import linear_model

4      from sklearn import model_selection

5      from sklearn.metrics import classification_report

6      from sklearn.metrics import confusion_matrix

7      from sklearn.metrics import accuracy_score

8      import matplotlib.pyplot as plt
```

9   import seaborn as sb

10   %matplotlib inline

We read the CSV file (for simplicity, it is considered to be in the same directory as the .ipynb notebook file) and assign it via Pandas to the variable dataframe. Using the dataframe.head () method, we see the first five records on the screen.

1 dataframe = pd.read_csv(r"usuarios_win_mac_lin.csv")

2 dataframe.head()

	A	B	C	D	E
1	duration ▾	pages ▾	actions ▾	value ▾	class ▾
2	7	2	4	8	2
3	21	2	6	6	2
4	57	2	4	4	2
5	101	3	6	12	2
6	109	2	6	12	2

Next, we call the dataframe.describe () method that will give us some basic statistical information on our data set. The Average, the standard deviation, minimum, and maximum values of each characteristic.

1 dataframe.describe()

Then we will analyze how many results we have of each type using the group by function, and we see that we have 86 "Class 0" users, which is Windows, 40 Mac users, and 44 Linux users.

1   print(dataframe.groupby('class').size())

```
clase
0      86
1      40
2      44
dtype: int64
```

Data Visualization

Before starting to process the data set, we will make some visualizations that can often help us to understand better the characteristics of the information we work with and its correlation.

First, we visualize in history format the four Input Features with names «duration», «pages», »actions», and «value» we can see graphically between which values their minimum and maximum are understood and in which intervals they concentrate the highest density of records.

```
1       dataframe.drop(['clase'],1).hist()

2       plt.show()
```

And we can also interrelate the peer inputs to see how colors linearly concentrate user exits: Windows Operating System in blue, Macintosh in green, and Linux in red.

And we can also interrelate the peer inputs, to see how user exits are linearly concentrated by colors: Windows Operating System in blue, Macintosh in green and Linux in red.

```
1        sb.pairplot(dataframe.dropna(),
hue='class',size=4,vars=["duration",
"pages","actions","values"],kind='reg')
```

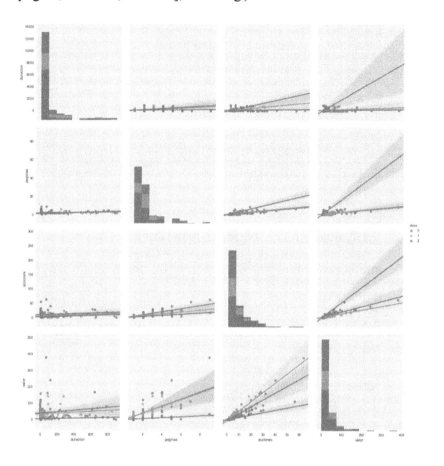

We Create the Logistic Regression Model

Now we load the variables of the 4 input columns in X excluding the «class» column with the drop () method. Instead we add the column "class" in the variable y. We run X.shape to check the size of our matrix with input data of 170 records by 4 columns.

```
1        X = np.array(dataframe.drop(['class'],1))
```

```
2      y = np.array(dataframe['class'])

3      X.shape
```

(170, 4)

And we create our model and make it fit (fit) to our set of inputs X and outputs 'and'.

```
1      model = linear_model.LogisticRegression()

2      model.fit(X,y)

<
```

p class = »»> LogisticRegression (C = 1.0, class_weight = None, dual = False, fit_intercept = True,

intercept_scaling = 1, max_iter = 100, multi_class = 'ovr', n_jobs = 1,

penalty = 'l2 ', random_state = None, solver = 'liblinear', tol = 0.0001,

verbose = 0, warm_start = False)

Once our model is compiled, we make it classify our entire set of X inputs using the "predict (X)" method, and we review some of its outputs and see that it matches the actual outputs of our CSV file.

```
1      predictions = model.predict(X)

2      print(predictions)[0:5]
```

[2 2 2 2 2]

And we confirm how good our model was using the model.score () that gives us the average accuracy of the predictions, in our case of 77%.

```
1    model.score(X,y)

     0.77647058823529413
```

Validation of our Model

Good practice in Machine Learning is to subdivide our set of input data into a training set and another to validate the model (which is not used during training and therefore, the machine is unknown). This will avoid problems in which our algorithm may fail to "overgeneralize" knowledge.

To do this, we subdivide our input data randomly (mixed) using 80% of training records and 20% to validate.

```
1    validation_size = 0.20

2    seed = 7

3    X_train, X_validation, Y_train, Y_validation =
     model_selection.train_test_split(X, y,
     test_size=validation_size, r    andom_state=seed)
```

We recompile our Logistic Regression model but this time only with 80% of the input data and calculate the new scoring that now gives us 74%.

```
1    name='Logistic Regression'

2    kfold = model_selection.KFold(n_splits=10,
     random_state=seed)
```

```
3      cv_results =
model_selection.cross_val_score(model, X_train, Y_train,
cv=kfold, scoring='accuracy')

4      msg = "%s: %f (%f)" % (name, cv_results.mean(),
cv_results.std())

5      print(msg)
```

Logistic Regression: 0.743407 (0.115752)

And now we make the predictions - in reality classification - using our "cross validation set", that is, the subset we had set aside. In this case we see that the hits were 85% but we must bear in mind that the data size was small.

```
1      predictions = model.predict(X_validation)

2      print(accuracy_score(Y_validation, predictions))
       0.852941176471
```

Finally we see on screen the "confusion matrix" where it shows how many wrong results it had of each class (those that are not on the diagonal), for example predicted 3 users who were Mac as Windows users and predicted 2 Linux users who really were Windows

Model Results Report

```
1      print(confusion_matrix(Y_validation, predictions))

       [[16   0   2]
        [ 3   3   0]
        [ 0   0  10]]
```

We can also see the classification report with our Validation set. In our case, we see that 18 windows, six mac, and 10 Linux records (total of 34 records) were used as "support." We can see the accuracy with which each class was successful, and we see that, for example, Macintosh had three successes and three failures (0.5 recall). The assessment that should be taken into account here is that of F1-score, which takes into account accuracy and recall. The average of F1 is 84% , which is not bad.

```
1 print(classification_report(Y_validation, predictions))
```

Classification (or prediction) of New Values

As the last step in the project, we will invent the navigation input data of a fictional user that has these values:

- Time Duration: 10

- Pages visited: 3

- Actions when browsing: 5

- Rating: 9

We test it on our model and see that it classifies it as a type 2 user, that is, Linux.

```
1     X_new = pd.DataFrame({'duration': [10], 'pages':
[3], 'actions': [5], 'values': [9]})

2     model.predict(X_new)

      array ([2])
```

I recommend you to play and vary these values to obtain Windows or Macintosh users.

In this section, the three classes are balanced, but what happens if I have data imbalance? Let's explore what to do in such a situation!

Classification with Unbalanced Data

- *Counteract problems with unbalanced classes*

- *Strategies to solve data imbalance in Python with the imbalanced-learn library.*

What are the problems of the classification of unbalanced classes? (imbalanced data)

In the classification problems where we have to label, for example, between "spam" or "not spam" or between multiple categories (car, ship, plane) we usually find that in our training data set we have some of the kinds of Sample is a "minority" class, that is, of which we have very few samples. This causes an imbalance in the data that we will use for the training of our machine.

An undeniable case is in the Health area where we usually find data sets with thousands of records with "negative" patients and a few positive cases; that is, they suffer from the disease we want to classify.

Other examples are usually Fraud Detection, where we have many samples of "honest" clients and few cases labeled as fraudulent. Or in a marketing funnel, where we typically have 2% of customer data that "buys" or executes some action (CTA) that we want to predict.

How does Unbalanced Data affect Us?

It usually affects algorithms in their process of generalizing information and harming minority classes. This sounds quite reasonable: if we give 990 photos of kittens and only 10 of dogs to a neural network, we cannot pretend that it can differentiate one class from another. Most likely, the network will answer "your picture is a cat" since it had a success of 99% in its training phase.

Metrics and Confusion Matrix

As I said, if we measure the effectiveness of our model by the number of successes it had, only considering the majority class, can we be having a false sense that the model works well?

To understand this a little better, we will use the so-called «Matrix Confusion» that will help us understand the outputs of our machine.

And from here come new metrics: precision and recall.

Let's look at the Confusion matrix with the example of dog and cat predictions by putting the values listed below:

Correct true positive for class 1 = 990

Wrong false positive for class 2 = 0

Wrong false positive for class 1 = 10

Correct true positive for class 2 = 0

Brief Explanation of these Metrics.

The Accuracy of the model is the total number of correct predictions divided by the total number of predictions. In this case, it gives 99% when we have not been able to identify any dog.

The Accuracy of a class defines how reliable a model is in responding if a point belongs to that class. For the cat class, it will be 99%; however, for the dog class, it will be 0%.

The Recall of a class expresses how well the model can detect that class. For cats, it will be 1 and for dogs 0.

The F1 Score of a class is given by the average harmony of precision and recall (2 x precision x recall / (precision + recall)) let's say that it combines precision and recall in a single metric. In our case, I would give zero for dogs!

We have four possible cases for each class:

- High precision and high recall: the model handles that class perfectly

- High precision and low recall: the model does not detect the class very well, but when it does, it is highly reliable.

- Low accuracy and high recall: The class detects the class well but also includes samples from other classes.

- Low accuracy and low recall: The model fails to classify the class correctly.

When we have a dataset with imbalance, it is often the case that we obtain a high precision value in the Majority class and a low recall in the Minority class.

Let's go to the Exercise with Python!

We will use the Credit Card Fraud Detection data set from the Kaggle website. They are 66 MB that will decompress 150MB. We will use the creditcard.csv file. This dataset consists of 285,000 rows with 31 columns (features).

As the information is private, we do not know what the features mean and are named as V1, V2, V3, etc. except for the Time and Amount columns (the amount of the transaction).

And our classes are 0 and 1 corresponding to "Normal transaction" or "There was Fraud." As you can imagine, the data set is very unbalanced, and we will have very few samples labeled as a fraud.

I must also say that we will not focus so much on the choice of the model or its configuration and tuning, but we will focus on applying the various strategies to improve the results despite the imbalance of classes.

Technical Requirements

We will need to have Python 3.6 in the system, and as we will do in a Jupyter Notebook, I recommend having Anaconda installed.

Install the Imbalanced Learn library from the command line with: (all documentation on the official website imbalancedlearn: https://imbalanced-learn.readthedocs.io/en/stable/)

```
1      pip install -U imbalanced-learn
```

Let's look at the dataset.

Exploratory Analysis to Check the Imbalance between Classes

```
1       import pandas as pd

2       import numpy as np

3       import matplotlib.pyplot as plt

4       import seaborn as sns

5

6       from sklearn.metrics import confusion_matrix

7       from sklearn.metrics import classification_report

8       from sklearn.model_selection import train_test_split

9       from sklearn.linear_model import LogisticRegression

10      from sklearn.decomposition import PCA

11      from sklearn.tree import DecisionTreeClassifier

12

13      from pylab import rcParams

14

15      from imblearn.under_sampling import NearMiss

16      from imblearn.over_sampling import RandomOverSampler

17      from imblearn.combine import SMOTETomek

18      from imblearn.ensemble import BalancedBaggingClassifier

19

20      from collections import Counter
```

After importing the libraries that we will use, we load the dataframe with pandas and see the first rows:

```
1    df = pd.read_csv("creditcard.csv") # read in data
     downloaded to the local directory

2    df.head(n=5)
```

Let's see how many rows we have and how many there are of each class:

```
1    print(df.shape)

2    print(pd.value_counts(df['Class'], sort = True))

     (284807, 31)

     0 284315

     1 492
```

Name: Class, dtype: int64

We see that there are 284,807 rows and only 492 are the minority class with cases of fraud. They represent 0.17% of the samples.

```
1    count_classes = pd.value_counts(df['Class'], sort =
     True)

2    count_classes.plot(kind = 'bar', rot=0)

3    plt.xticks(range(2), LABELS)

4    plt.title("Frequency by observation number")

5    plt.xlabel("Class")

6    plt.ylabel("Number of Observations");
```

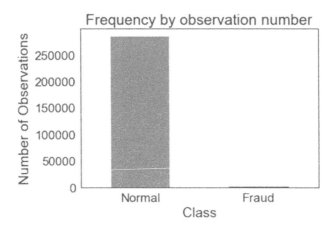

Do you get to see the tiny red line that represents the cases of Fraud? There are very few samples!

Strategies for Handling Unbalanced Data:

We have various strategies to try to improve the situation. We will comment briefly and move on to the action (to the code!) Below.

1. **Model Parameter Adjustment:** It consists of adjusting parameters or metrics of the algorithm itself to try to balance the minority class penalizing the majority class during training. Examples with weight adjustment in trees, also in logistic regression, we have the class_weight = "balanced" parameter that we will use in this example. Not all algorithms have these possibilities. In neural networks, for example, we could adjust the Loss metric to penalize the majority classes.

2. **Modify the Dataset:** we can eliminate samples from the majority class to reduce it and try to balance the situation. It has as "dangerous" that we can dispense with essential samples, which provide information and therefore make the

model worse. So to select which samples to remove, we should follow some criteria. We could also add new rows with the same values of minority classes, for example, quadruple our 492 rows. But this does not help much, and we can lead the model to fall into overfitting.

3. **Artificial samples:** we can try to create synthetic samples (not identical) using various algorithms that try to follow the trend of the minority group. Depending on the method, we can improve the results. The dangerous thing about creating synthetic samples is that we can alter the "natural" distribution of that class and confuse the model in its classification.

4. **Balanced Ensemble Methods:** It uses the advantages of assembling methods, that is, training various models and getting the final result together (for example, "voting"), but it makes sure to take balanced training samples.

Let's apply these techniques one by one to our code and see the results.

BUT... before we start, we will execute the "Unbalanced" Logistic Regression model, to have a "baseline," that is, some metrics against which we can compare and see if we improve.

Testing the "Dry" Model - Without Strategies

```
1      #define our tags and features
2      y = df ['Class']
3      X = df.drop ('Class', axis = 1)
```

```
4       # We divide into training and test sets

5       X_train, X_test, y_train, y_test = train_test_split (X,
y, train_size = 0.7)

6

7       #create a function that creates the model that we will
use every time

8       def run_model (X_train, X_test, y_train, y_test):

9       clf_base = LogisticRegression (C = 1.0, penalty =
'l2', random_state = 1, solver = "newton-cg")

10      clf_base.fit (X_train, y_train)

11      return clf_base

12

13      #execute the "as is" model

14      model = run_model (X_train, X_test, y_train, y_test)

15

16      #definimos works to show the results

17      def show_results (y_test, pred_y):

18      conf_matrix = confusion_matrix (y_test, pred_y)

19      plt.figure (figsize = (12, 12))

20      sns.heatmap (conf_matrix, xticklabels = LABELS,
yticklabels = LABELS, annot = True, fmt = "d");

21      plt.title ("Confusion matrix")

22      plt.ylabel ('True class')
```

```
23      plt.xlabel ('Predicted class')

24      plt.show ()

25      print (classification_report (y_test, pred_y))

26

27      pred_y = model.predict (X_test)

28      show_results (y_test, pred_y)
```

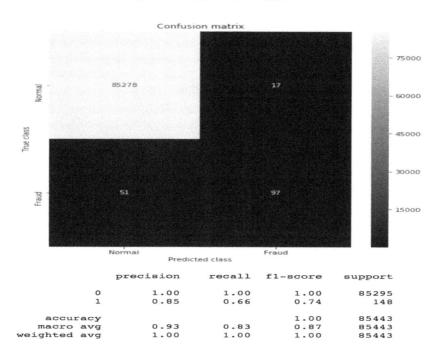

	precision	recall	f1-score	support
0	1.00	1.00	1.00	85295
1	0.85	0.66	0.74	148
accuracy			1.00	85443
macro avg	0.93	0.83	0.87	85443
weighted avg	1.00	1.00	1.00	85443

Here we see the confusion matrix and in class 2 (which is what we are interested in detecting) we see 51 failures and 97 hits giving a 0.66 recall and it is the value we want to improve. It is also interesting to note that in the column of f1-score we get very good results BUT they really should not deceive us ... they are reflecting a partial reality. The truth is that our model is not able to correctly detect fraud cases.

59

Strategy: Penalty to Compensate

We will use an additional parameter in the Logistic Regression model where we indicate weight = "balanced" and with this the algorithm will be in charge of balancing the minority class during training. Let's see:

```
1    def run_model_balanced(X_train, X_test, y_train,
     y_test):
2    clf
     =LogisticRegression(C=1.0,penalty='l2',random_state=1,sol
     ver="newto    n-cg",class_weight="balanced")
3    clf.fit(X_train, y_train)
4    return clf
5
6    model = run_model_balanced(X_train, X_test,
     y_train, y_test)
7    pred_y = model.predict(X_test)
8    show_results (y_test, pred_y)
```

Now we see a NOTABLE IMPROVEMENT! In class 2 - which indicates if there was fraud - 137 samples were successful and failed in 11, giving a recall of 0.93 !! and just by adding a parameter to the model. Also, note that in the f1-score column, it would appear that the results had "worsened" ... when we are improving the detection of fraudulent cases.

The False Positives increase and 1890 samples have indeed been labeled as Fraudulent when they were not, but you think, what does the banking company prefer? Have to review these cases manually or fail to detect the true cases of fraud?

Let's continue with more methods:

Strategy: Subsampling in the Majority Class

What we will do is use an algorithm to reduce the majority class. We will do it using an algorithm that makes the k-nearest neighbor similar to select which ones to eliminate. Let us note that we reduce beastly from 199,020 samples of zero class (most) and become 688. And With those samples we train the model.

```
1       us = NearMiss(ratio=0.5, n_neighbors=3, version=2,
        random_state=1)

2       X_train_res, y_train_res = us.fit_sample(X_train,
y_train)

3

4       print ("Distribution before resampling
        {}".format(Counter(y_train)))

5       print ("Distribution after resampling
        {}".format(Counter(y_train_res)))

6

7       model = run_model(X_train_res, X_test,
y_train_res, y_test)

8       pred_y = model.predict(X_test)

9       show_results (y_test, pred_y)
```

Distribution after resampling Counter ({0: 199020, 1: 344})

Distribution after resampling Counter ({0: 688, 1: 344})

We also see that we get an excellent result with a recall of 0.93, although at the cost of increasing false positives.

Strategy: Minority Class Oversampling

In this case, we will create new "synthetic" samples of the minority class. Using RandomOverSampler. And we see that we went from 344 fraud samples to 99,510.

```
1 os = RandomOverSampler(ratio=0.5)
2 X_train_res, y_train_res = os.fit_sample(X_train, y_train)
3
4 print ("Distribution before resampling {}".format(Counter(y_train)))
5 print ("Distribution labels after resampling {}".format(Counter(y_train_res)))
6
7 model = run_model(X_train_res, X_test, y_train_res, y_test)
8 pred_y = model.predict(X_test)
9 show_results (y_test, pred_y)
```

We have a 0.89 recall for class 2, and the False positives are 838. Not bad.

Strategy: We Combine Resampling with Smote-Tomek

Now we will try a widely used technique that consists of simultaneously applying a subsampling algorithm and an oversampling algorithm at the same time to the dataset. In this case, we will use SMOTE for oversampling: look for nearby neighboring points and add points "in a straight line" between them. And we will use Tomek for undersampling that removes those of different kinds that are closest neighbors and let us see the boundary decision (the border zone of our classes).

```
1       os_us = SMOTETomek(ratio=0.5)

2       X_train_res, y_train_res = os_us.fit_sample(X_train,
y_train)

3

4       print ("Distribution before resampling
{}".format(Counter(y_train)))

5       print ("Distribution after resampling
{}".format(Counter(y_train_res)))

6

7       model = run_model(X_train_res, X_test,
y_train_res, y_test)

8       pred_y = model.predict(X_test)

9       mostrar_resultados(y_test, pred_y)
```

1   Distribution labels before resampling Counter({0: 199020, 1: 344})
 Distribution after resampling Counter({0: 198194, 1: 98684})

In this case, we still have a pretty good 0.85 recall of class 2, and we see that the False positives of class 1 are quite a few, 325 (out of 85295 samples).

Strategy: Rolling Model Assembly

For this strategy we will use an Assembly Classifier that uses Bagging and the model will be a DecisionTree. Let's see how it behaves:

```
1
        bbc=BalancedBaggingClassifier(base_estimator=DecisionTreeClassifier(),

2                       sampling_strategy='auto',

3                       replacement=False,

4                       random_state=0)

5

6 #Train the classifier.

7       bbc.fit(X_train, y_train)

8       pred_y = bbc.predict(X_test)

9       show_results (y_test, pred_y)
```

It is not bad either. We always see improvement concerning the initial model with a 0.88 recall for cases of fraud.

Results of the Strategies

Let's see in a table, ordered from best to worst the results obtained.

Column1	algorithm	precision	recall	overall
1	Penalty	1.0	0.93	0.965
2	NearMiss Subsampling	1.0	0.93	0.965
3	Random Oversampling	1.0	0.89	0.945
5	Ensemble	1.0	0.88	0.940
4	Smote Tomek	1.0	0.85	0.925
0	Logistic Regression	1.0	0.66	0.830

We understand that in our case, the Penalization and Subsampling strategies give us the best result, each with a recall of 0.93.

But let's keep this: With any of the techniques we apply, we IMPROVE the initial Logistic Regression model, which achieved a 0.66 recall for the Fraud class. And let's not forget that there is a tremendous imbalance of classes in the dataset!

IMPORTANT: this does not mean that you always have to apply Penalization or NearMiss Subsampling! It will depend on the case, the imbalance, and the model (in this case, we use logistic regression, but it could be another!).

It is widespread to find datasets with unbalanced classes; in fact the strangest thing would be to find well-balanced datasets.

The most frequent question I receive is "how to do when I have a few samples of a class?". My first and common sense answer is, «Go out and get more samples!» But the reality is that it is not always possible to get more data from minority classes (such as in Health Cases).

Chapter Summary

In this chapter, we saw several strategies to follow to combat this problem: eliminate samples from the majority set, create synthetic samples with some criteria, assembly, and penalty.

We also review the Confusion Matrix and understand that metrics can be misleading; if we look at our successes only, we may think we have a good classifier when it is failing.

Finally, throughout this chapter, we saw how to create a Logistic Regression model in Python to be able to classify the Operating System of users based on their navigation features on a website. From this example, it can be extended to other types of tasks that may arise during our work, in which we must classify results in discrete values. If we were to predict continuous values, we must apply Linear Regression.

CHAPTER
FOUR

K-Means in Python

K-Means is an algorithm unsupervised for Clustering. It is used when we have a lot of unlabeled data. The objective of this algorithm is to find «K» groups (clusters) among the raw data. In this chapter, we will review its basics and see a step-by-step example in python.

How K-Means Works

The algorithm works iteratively to assign to each «point» (the rows of our input set form a coordinate) one of the «K» groups based on their characteristics. They are grouped based on the similarity of their features (the columns). As a result of executing the algorithm, we will have:

- The "centroids" of each group that will be "coordinates" of each of the K sets that will be used to label new samples.

- Labels for the training data set. Each label belongs to one of the K groups formed.

The groups are defined in an "organic" way that is to say that their position is adjusted in each iteration of the process until the algorithm converges. Once the centroids are found, we must analyze them to see what their unique characteristics are, compared to that of the other groups. These groups are the tags generated by the algorithm.

K-Means Use Cases

The K-means Clustering algorithm is one of the most used to find hidden groups or suspected in theory about an unlabeled data set. This can serve to confirm - or banish - some theory that we had assumed of our data.

And it can also help us discover amazing relationships between data sets, which we would not have recognized manually. Once the algorithm has executed and obtained the tags, it will be easy to classify new values or samples among the groups obtained.

Some use cases are:

- Segmentation by Behavior - relate a user's shopping cart, their action times, and profile information.

- Inventory Categorization - grouping products by sales activity

- Detect anomalies or suspicious activities: according to the behavior on a website, recognize a troll - or a bot - of a regular user.

Input Data for K-Means

The "features" or characteristics that we will use as inputs to apply the k-means algorithm should be numerical, continuous as much as possible. In the case of categorical values (e.g., Male / Female or Science Fiction, Terror, Novel, etc.) you can try to pass it to a numerical value, but it is not recommended because there is no "real distance" - as in the case of genres of movie or books.

It is also recommended that the values used are standardized, maintaining the same scale. In some cases, percentage data also works better than absolute ones. It is not convenient to use features that are correlated or scalar from others. Remember the seven steps to Machine Learning.

The K-means Algorithm

The algorithm uses an iterative process in which the groups are adjusted to produce the final result. To execute the algorithm, we must pass as input the data set and a value of K. The data set will be the characteristics or features for each point. The initial positions of the K centroids will be randomly assigned from any point in the input data set. Then it is iterated in two steps:

1   Data Assignment Step

In this step, each "row" of our data set is assigned to the nearest centroid based on the Euclidean square distance. The following formula is used (where dist () is the standard Euclidean distance):

$$\underset{c_i \in C}{\arg\min} \; dist(c_i, \; x)^2$$

2   Step Centroid update

In this step, the centroids of each group are recalculated. This is done by taking an average of all the points assigned in the previous step.

$$c_i = \frac{1}{|S_i|} \sum_{x_i \in S_i} x_i$$

The algorithm iterates between these steps until a stop criterion is met:

* if there are no changes in the points assigned to the groups,

* or if the sum of the distances is minimized,

* or a maximum number of iterations is reached.

The algorithm converges to a result that can be the local optimum, so it will be convenient to rerun more than once with random starting points to confirm if there is better output. Always remember to follow the seven steps to build AI

Choose the Value of K

This algorithm works by pre-selecting a value of K. To find the number of clusters in the data, we must execute the algorithm for a range of K values, see the results and compare characteristics of the groups obtained. In general, there is no exact way to determine the K value, but it can be estimated with acceptable accuracy by following the following technique:

One of the metrics used to compare results is the average distance between the data points and their centroid. Since the value of the mean will decrease as we increase the value of K, we must use the average distance to the centroid as a function of K and find the "elbow point," where the rate of descent is "sharpened." Here we see an example graph:

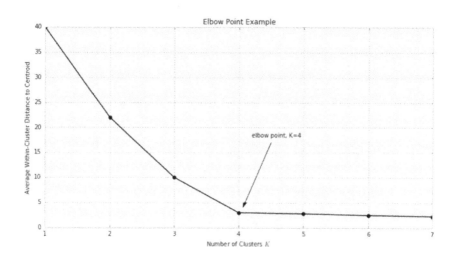

An Example of K-Means in Python with Sklearn

As an example, we will use a set of data that I obtained from my project, which analyzed the personality traits of Twitter users. I have leaked 140 "celebrities" from around the world in different areas: sports, singers, actors, etc. Based on a psychology methodology known as "Ocean: The Big Five," we have as input characteristics:

- user (the name on Twitter)

- «Op» = Openness to experience - degree of mental openness to new experiences, curiosity, art

- «Co» = Conscientiousness - degree of order, prolixity, organization

- «Ex» = Extraversion - degree of shyness, solitary or participation before the social group

- «Ag» = Agreeableness - degree of empathy with others, temperament

- «Ne» = Neuroticism, - degree of neuroticism, nervous, irritability, self-confidence.

- Wordcount - Average number of words used in your tweets

- Category - User work activity (actor, singer, etc.)

We will use the K-means algorithm to group these users - not because of their work activity - if not, because of their similarities in personality. Although we have eight input columns, we will only use three in this example, so that we can see the resulting groups in a three-dimensional graph - and its 2D projections.

But for real cases, we can use all the dimensions we need. One of the hypotheses we could have is: "All singers will have similar personality" (and so with each work item). Well, we will see if we try it, or on the contrary, the groups are not necessarily related to the activity of these Celebrities.

Requirements for the Project

We will need to have Python 2.7 or 3.5+. Better if we have installed a suite like Anaconda or Canopy (which work on Windows, Mac, and Linux). You can follow this tutorial, where I explain how to install your development environment. I suggest you create a Jupiter notebook to follow the exercise step by step and import a CSV input file. We will use scikit-learn, pandas, matplotlib, and numpy packages.

Implementing K-means in Python with Sklearn - Group Twitter Users According to their Personality with K-means

We will start importing the libraries that will assist us in executing the algorithm and graph.

```
1    import pandas as pd

2    import numpy as np

3    import matplotlib.pyplot as plt

4    import seaborn as sb

5    from sklearn.cluster import KMeans

6    from sklearn.metrics import
pairwise_distances_argmin_min

7

8    %matplotlib inline

9    from mpl_toolkits.mplot3d import Axes3D

10   plt.rcParams['figure.figsize'] = (16, 9)

11   plt.style.use('ggplot')
```

We import the csv file - to simplify, we assume that the file is in the same directory as the notebook - and we see the first 5 records of the tabulated file.

```
1 dataframe = pd.read_csv(r"analisis.csv")

2 dataframe.head()
```

We can also see a table of statistical information provided by Pandas dataframe:

he project contains nine different categories - labor activities, for example - which are:

1. Actor actress

2. Singer

3. Model

4. TV series

5. Radio

6. Technology

7. sports

8. Politics

9. Writer

To know how many records we have of each one we make:

```
1       print(dataframe.groupby('categoria').size())
```

Category

1	27
2	34
3	9
4	19
5	4
6	8

7	17
8	16
9	6

dtype: int64

As we see, we have 34 singers, 27 actors, 17 athletes, 16 politicians, etc.

Data Visualization

We will see our data graphically to get an idea of their dispersion:

1   dataframe.drop(['category'],1).hist()

2   plt.show()

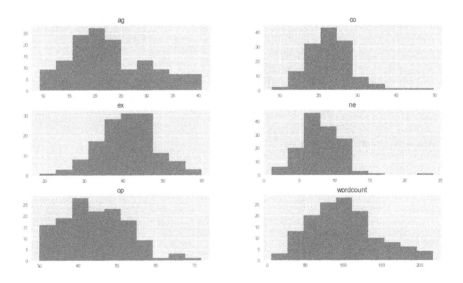

In this case we select 3 dimensions: op, ex and ag and cross them to see if they give us any clue of their grouping and the relationship with their categories.

```
1   sb.pairplot(dataframe.dropna(),hue='category',size=4,vars=["op","e
x","ag"],kin ='scatter')
```

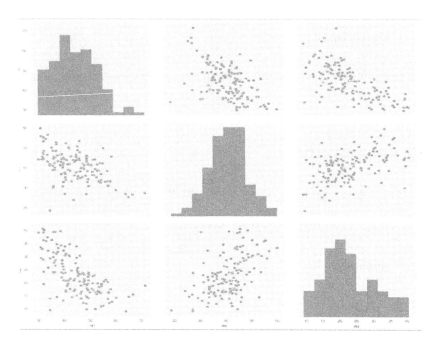

Reviewing the graph does not seem to make any sort of grouping or correlation between users and their categories.

We Define the Entrance

We specify the data structure that we will use to feed the algorithm. As you can see, we only load the op, ex and ag columns in our variable X.

```
1   X = np.array(dataframe[["op","ex","ag"]])

2   y = np.array(dataframe['categoria'])

3   X.shape
```

(140.3)

Now we will see a 3D graphic with 9 colors representing the categories.

```
1       fig = plt.figure()
2       ax = Axes3D(fig)
colors=['blue','red','green','blue','cyan','yellow','orange','black
','pink','brown','purple']
4       asignar=[]
5       for row in y:
6       asignar.append(colors[row])
7       ax.scatter(X[:, 0], X[:, 1], X[:, 2], c=asignar,s=60)
```

We will see if with K-means, we can "paint" this same graph in another way, with differentiated clusters.

Get the K Value

We are going to find the value of K by graphing and trying to find the "elbow point" that we mentioned before. This is our result:

```
1    Nc = range(1, 20)

2    kmeans = [KMeans(n_clusters=i) for i in Nc]

3    kmeans

4    score = [kmeans[i].fit(X).score(X) for i in
     range(len(kmeans))]

5    score

6    plt.plot(Nc,score)

7    plt.xlabel('Number of Clusters')

8    plt.ylabel('Score')

9    plt.title('Elbow Curve')

10   plt.show()
```

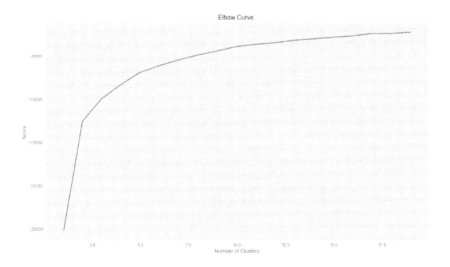

The curve really is quite "soft." I consider 5 a good number for K. In your opinion it could be another.

We execute K-Means

We execute the algorithm for 5 clusters and obtain the labels and the centroids.

```
1    kmeans = KMeans(n_clusters=5).fit(X)

2    centroids = kmeans.cluster_centers_

3    print(centroids)
```

```
[[ 49.80086386   40.8972579    17.48224326]
 [ 39.63830586   44.75784737   25.86962057]
 [ 58.58657531   31.02839375   15.6120435 ]
 [ 34.5303535    48.01261321   35.01749504]
 [ 42.302263     33.65449587   20.812626  ]]
```

Now we will see this in a 3D graph with colors for the groups and we will see if they differ: (the stars mark the center of each cluster)

```
1    # Predicting the clusters

2    labels = kmeans.predict(X)

3    # Getting the cluster centers

4    C = kmeans.cluster_centers_

5    colors=['red','green','blue','cyan','yellow']

6    asignar=[]

7    for row in labels:

8    asignar.append(colors[row])

9
```

```
10      fig = plt.figure()

11      ax = Axes3D(fig)

12      ax.scatter(X[:, 0], X[:, 1], X[:, 2], c=asignar,s=60)

13      ax.scatter(C[:, 0], C[:, 1], C[:, 2], marker='*',
c=colors, s=1000)
```

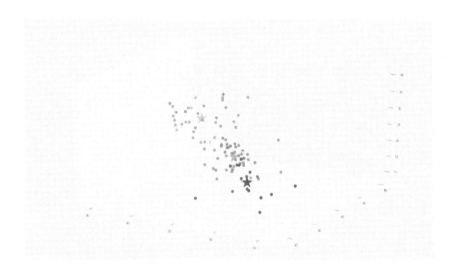

Here we can see that the K-Means Algorithm with K = 5 has grouped
the 140 Twitter users by their personality, taking into account the 3
dimensions we use: Openess, Extraversion and Agreeablenes. It
seems that there is not necessarily a relationship in the groups with
their Celebrity activities.

We will make 3 graphs in 2 dimensions with the projections from our
3D graph to help us visualize the groups and their classification:

```
1       # Getting the values and plotting it

2       f1 = dataframe['op'].values

3       f2 = dataframe['ex'].values
```

4

5   plt.scatter(f1, f2, c=asignar, s=70)

6   plt.scatter(C[:, 0], C[:, 1], marker='*', c=colors, s=1000)

7   plt.show()

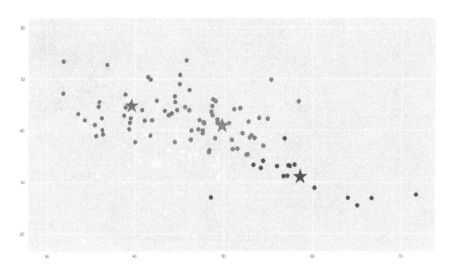

1   # Getting the values and plotting it

2   f1 = dataframe['op'].values

3   f2 = dataframe['ag'].values

4

5   plt.scatter(f1, f2, c=asignar, s=70)

6   plt.scatter(C[:, 0], C[:, 1], marker='*', c=colors, s=1000)

7   plt.show()

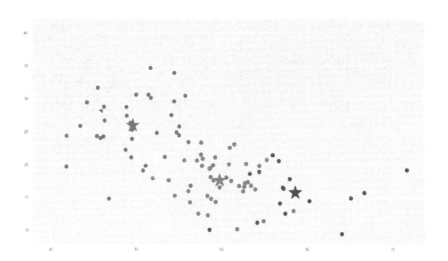

1   f1 = dataframe['ex'].values

2   f2 = dataframe['ag'].values

3

4   plt.scatter(f1, f2, c=asignar, s=70)

5   plt.scatter(C[:, 0], C[:, 1], marker='*', c=colors, s=1000)

6   plt.show()

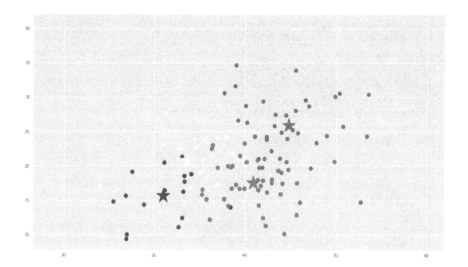

In these graphs we see that the groups are quite well differentiated.

We can see each of the clusters how many users it has:

1   copy = pd.DataFrame ()

2   copy ['user'] = dataframe ['user']. values

3   copy ['category'] = dataframe ['category']. values

4   copy ['label'] = labels;

5   amountGroup = pd.DataFrame ()

6   Quantity Group ['color'] = colors

7   quantityGroup ['quantity'] = copy.groupby ('label'). size ()

8   group quantity

	Color	Quantity
0	red	42
1	green	33
2	blue	16
3	cyan	27
4	yellow	22

And we can see the diversity in each work item. For example, in group 0 (red), we see that there are all the work activities although they predominate from activity 1 and 2 corresponding to Actors and Singers with 11 and 15 celebrities.

```
1      group_referrer_index = copy ['label'] == 0
2      group_referrals = copy [group_referrer_index]
3
4      diversityGroup = pd.DataFrame ()
5      diversity Group ['category'] = [0,1,2,3,4,5,6,7,8,9]
6      diversityGroup ['quantity'] =
group_referrals.groupby ('category'). size ()
7      diversity group
```

	Category	Quantity
0	0	NaN
1	1	11.0
2	2	15.0
3	3	6.0
4	4	3.0
5	5	1.0
6	6	2.0
7	7	2.0
8	8	1.0
9	9	1.0

In category 3 "models," there are 6 out of a total of 9.

We will look for the users that are closest to the centroids of each group that we could say that have the characteristic personality traits that represent each cluster:

```
1       #we see the representative of the group, the user
close to your center

2       closest, _ = pairwise_distances_argmin_min
(kmeans.cluster_centers_, X)

3       closest
```

array ([21, 107, 82, 80, 91]) #position in the user array

```
1       users = dataframe ['user']. values

2       for row in closest:

3               print (users [row])
```

<

p style = »padding-left: 30px;»> angelinajolie

Bill_Clinton_

TigerWood

TomCruise

BradPit

In the centers, we see that we have a model, a politician, a TV presenter, a Radio announcer, and an athlete, for example.

Sort New Samples

And finally we can group and tag new twitter users with their characteristics and classify them. We see the example with the user of David Guetta and he returns that it belongs to group 1 (green).

```
1       X_new = np.array ([[45.92,57.74,15.66]]) #davidguetta

2

3       new_labels = kmeans.predict (X_new)

4       print (new_labels)
```

[one]

Summary of the Chapter

The K-means algorithm will help us create clusters when we have large groups of unlabeled data when we want to try to discover new relationships between features or to test or decline hypotheses we have of our business.

Attention: There may be cases in which there are no natural groups or clusters that contain a valid reason for being. Although K-means will always provide us with «k clusters,» it will be in our discretion to recognize their usefulness or to review our features and discard those that do not work or get new ones. Also, keep in mind that in this example, we are using the Euclidean distance as a measure of similarity between features, but we can use various other functions that could yield better results (such as Manhattan, Levenshtein, Mahalanobis, etc.).

We have seen a description of the algorithm, applications, and a step-by-step python example.

CHAPTER

FIVE

Decision Tree in Python - Classification and Prediction

In this chapter we will quickly describe what the decision trees used in Machine Learning consist of and how they work, and we will focus on a fun example in Python in which we will analyze the singers and bands that achieved a number one position on the Billboard Hot 100 charts, and we will try to predict who will be the next Ed Sheeran by force of Artificial Intelligence. We will make Graphs that will help us visualize the input data and a graph to interpret the tree that we will create with the Scikit-Learn package. Let's start!

What is a Decision Tree?

Decision trees are graphic representations of possible solutions to a decision based on certain conditions, it is one of the most used supervised learning algorithms in machine learning and can perform classification or regression tasks (an acronym for CART). Understanding how it works is usually simple and yet very powerful.

We use decision tree structures constantly in our daily lives without realizing:

Rains? => carry umbrella. Sunny? => Wear sunglasses. I'm tired? => drink coffee. (IF THIS THEN THAT decisions)

The decision trees have a first node called root (root), and then the other input attributes are broken down into two branches (they could be more, but we will not get into that now) posing a condition that may be true or false. Each node is forked in two, and they are subdivided again until they reach the leaves that are the final nodes, and that is equivalent to answers to the solution: Yes / No, Buy / Sell, or whatever we are classifying.

Another example is the popular riddle games:

1. Animal or vegetable? -Animal

2. Does it have four legs? -Yes

3. Does it bark? -Yes

4. -> It's a dog!

What is the Need to use the Tree Algorithm?

Suppose we have attributes such as Gender with values "male or female" and age in ranges: "under 18 or over 18" to make a decision. We could create a tree in which we divide first by gender and then subdivide by age. Or it could be the other way around: first by age and then by gender.

The algorithm is the one who analyzes the data and the outputs - that is why it is supervised! - Decide the best way to make the divisions (split) between nodes. It will take into account how to achieve a prediction (classification or regression) with a higher probability of success.

It seems simple, doesn't it? Let's think that if we have ten input attributes, each with two or more possible values, the combinations to decide the best tree would be hundreds or thousands. This is no longer a job to do by hand. And that is where this algorithm becomes essential because he will return the optimal tree for the most successful decision making from a probabilistic point of view.

How does a Decision Tree Work?

To obtain the optimal tree and evaluate each subdivision among all possible trees and get the root node and subsequent ones, the algorithm must measure the predictions achieved in some way and evaluate them to compare among all and obtain the best.

To measure and evaluate, it uses various functions; the best known and used is the " Gini Index " and " Information Gain " used by the so-called " entropy." The division of nodes will continue until we reach the maximum possible depth of the tree, or the nodes are limited to a minimum number of samples on each sheet. Next, we will describe very briefly each of the strategies named:

Gini Index:

It is used for attributes with continuous values (the price of a house). This cost function measures the "degree of impurity" of the nodes; that is, how messy or mixed the nodes are once divided. We must minimize that GINI index.

Information gain:

It is used for categorical attributes (as in men/women). This criterion attempts to estimate the information provided by each attribute based on the " information theory." To measure the randomness of the uncertainty of a random value of a variable "X," Entropy is defined.

By obtaining the entropy measure of each attribute, we can calculate the information gain of the tree. *We must maximize that gain.*

Example of Decision Tree with Python SKLearn Step by Step

For this project, we will try to create an original data set and try to make it fun while clearly explaining how the tree works. Let's start:

Requirements to do the Exercise

To perform this project, I recommend you use a Jupyter notebook with python code, and the Scikit learn library widely used in Data Science. I also recommend using the Anaconda suite. If you don't have it yet, you can read chapter 2 once again, where it shows step by step how to install the development environment.

Prediction of the «Billboard 100»: Which artist will reach the number one ranking?

From the attributes of singers and history of songs that reached Billboard 100 (US) in 2013 and 2014, we will create a tree that allows us to try to predict whether a new singer can reach number one.

Obtaining the Input Data

I used a python code to make a webscraping of a public website "Ultimate Music Database" with historical information of the Billboard that I obtained from this article: "Analyzing the billboard hot 100". Then I completed attributes using the Deezer API (duration of the songs), the Gracenote API (genre and rhythm of the songs).

I finally added several artist birth dates by hand using Wikipedia that I had not gotten with the Ultimate Music Database. Some artists were left without completing their date of birth and with value 0. We will see how to overcome this obstacle by treating the data.

To start, we import the libraries that we will use and review their input attributes:

```
1     # Imports needed for the script

2     import numpy as np

3     import pandas as pd

4     import seaborn as sb

5     import matplotlib.pyplot as plt

6     % matplotlib inline

7     plt.rcParams ['figure.figsize'] = (16, 9)

8     plt.style.use ('ggplot')

9     from sklearn import tree

10    from sklearn.metrics import accuracy_score
```

```
11      from sklearn.model_selection import KFold

12      from sklearn.model_selection import cross_val_score

13      from IPython.display import Image as PImage

14      from subprocess import check_call

15      from PIL import Image, ImageDraw, ImageFont
```

If you are missing any of them, remember that you can install it with the Anaconda environment or with the Pip tool.

Initial Exploratory Analysis

Now let's see how many columns and records we have:

```
1       artists_billboard.shape
```

This returns us (635.11); that is, we have 11 columns (features) and 635 rows of data. Let's take a look at the first records to get a better idea of the content:

```
1       artists_billboard.head()
```

	id	title	artist	mood	tempo	genre	artist_type	chart_date	durationSeg	top	Birth Year
0	0	Small Town Throwdown	BRANTLEY GILBERT featuring JUSTIN MOORE & THOM...	Brooding	Medium Tempo	Traditional	Male	20140628	191.0	0	1975.0
1	1	Bang Bang	JESSIE J, ARIANA GRANDE & NICKI MINAJ	Energizing	Medium Tempo	Pop	Female	20140816	368.0	0	1989.0
2	2	Timber	PITBULL featuring KE$HA	Excited	Medium Tempo	Urban	Mixed	20140118	223.0	1	1993.0
3	3	Sweater Weather	THE NEIGHBOURHOOD	Brooding	Medium Tempo	Alternative & Punk	Male	20140104	206.0	0	1989.0
4	4	Automatic	MIRANDA LAMBERT	Yearning	Medium Tempo	Traditional	Female	20140301	232.0	0	0.0

We see that we have: Title of the song, artist, "mood" or mood of that song, tempo, genre, Type of artist, the date on which it appeared on the billboard (for example 20140628 is equivalent to June 28, 2014).

The TOP column would be our label, in which 1 appears if it reached Billboard number one or 0 if it did not reach it and the artist's birth year. We see that many of the columns contain certain information.

The durationSeg column contains the duration in seconds of the song, being a continuous value but which should be categorical later.

We will make some visualizations to understand our data better.

First, let's group records to see how many reached number one and how many did not:

```
1       artists_billboard.groupby('top').size()
```

returns us:

    top

0 494

1 141

In other words, we have 494 songs that did not reach the top and 141 that reached number one. This means that we have an UNBALANCED number of labels with 1 and 0. We will consider it when creating the tree.

Our labels that indicate 0-I do not reach the Top and 1-I reach the number one Billboard are unbalanced. We must solve this problem.

Let's see how many records there are of type of artist, "mood", tempo and genre of songs:

1
      sb.factorplot('artist_type',data=artists_billboard,kind="count
")

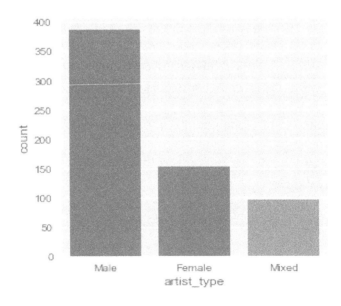

Here we see that we have more than twice as many males as female artists and about 100 mixed song records.

1   sb.factorplot('mood',data=artists_billboard,kind="count", aspect=3)

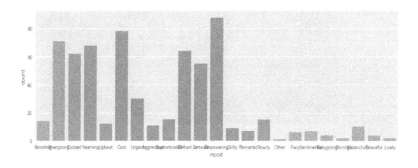

We see that of 23 types of Mood, 7 stands out with high peaks. We also noticed that some moods are similar.

1

        sb.factorplot('tempo',data=artists_billboard,hue='top',kind=" count")

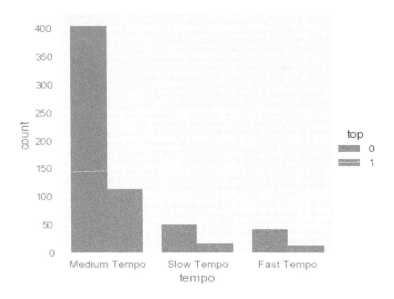

In this graph, we see that there are three types of Tempo: Medium, Slow, and Fast. The Medium times predominate, and it is also where we find more songs that have reached the Top 1 (in blue).

1   sb.factorplot ('genre', data = artists_billboard, kind = "count", aspect = 3)

Data Balancing: Few Artists Reach Number One

As we said before, we have no "balance" in the number of top and "non-top" tags of the songs because, in a year only about 5 or 6 songs achieve first place and remain for several weeks in that position. When I initially extracted the songs, I used 2014 and 2015 and had only 11 songs on the top of Billboard and 494 that did not arrive.

To try to balance the positive cases, I added only the TOPs from 2004 to 2013. With that, I got the values we have in the CSV file: they are

494 "non-top" and 141 top. Despite this, it is still unbalanced, and we could continue adding only TOP songs from previous years, but we will use a parameter (class_weight) of the decision tree algorithm to compensate for this difference.

Let's visualize the top and not top according to their dates in the Charts:

```
1      f1 = artists_billboard ['chart_date']. values
2      f2 = artists_billboard ['durationSeg']. values
3
4      colors = ['orange', 'blue'] # if not previously declared
5      size = [60,40] # if they were not previously declared
6
7      assign = []
8      assign2 = []
9      for index, row in artists_billboard.iterrows ():
10             assign.append (colors [row ['top']])
11             assign2.append (sizes [row ['top']])
12
13     plt.scatter (f1, f2, c = assign, s = sizes)
14     plt.axis ([20030101,20160101,0,600])
15     plt.show ()
```

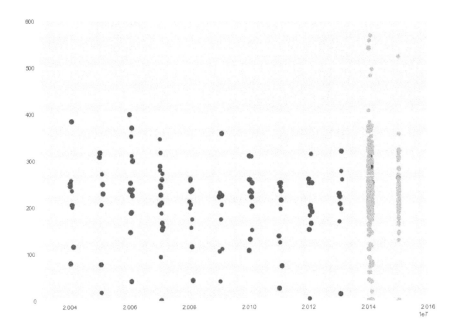

In our data set, songs were added that reached the top (in blue) from 2004 to 2013 to add to just 11 who had achieved it in 2014-2015.

We Prepare the Data

We will fix the problem of the years of birth that is at zero. The "feature" or feature that we want to obtain is: "knowing the singer's year of birth, calculate how old he was at the time of appearing on the Billboard." For example, an artist who was born in 1982 and appeared on the charts in 2012, was 30 years old.

First we are going to substitute the zeros of the column «Birth Year» with the value None -which is null in Python-.

```
1    def age_fix(year):

2        if year==0:

3            return None
```

```
4          return year

5

           artists_billboard['Birthyear']=artists_billboard.apply(
lambda x: age_fix(x['Birthyear']), axis=1);
```

Then we will calculate the ages in a new column "age_in_billboard" by subtracting the year of appearance (the first 4 characters of chart_date) to the year of birth. In the rows that were the year in None, we will result in age None.

```
1          def age_calculation (year, when):

2          cad = str (when)

3          moment = cad [: 4]

4          if year == 0.0:

5                    return None

6          return int (moment) - year

7

8          artists_billboard ['age_in_billboard'] =
artists_billboard.apply (lambda x: calculates_age (x
['Birthyear'], x ['chart_date']), axis = 1);
```

And finally we will assign random ages to the missing records: for this, we obtain the average age of our set (avg) and its standard deviation (std) - that is why we needed the ages in None - and we asked random values to the function that go from avg - std to avg + std. In our case they are ages between 21 and 37 years.

```
1       age_avg = artists_billboard ['age_in_billboard'].
mean ()

2       age_std = artists_billboard ['age_in_billboard']. std ()

3       age_null_count = artists_billboard
['age_in_billboard']. isnull (). sum ()

4       age_null_random_list = np.random.randint (age_avg
- age_std, age_avg + age_std, size = age_null_count)

5

6       withValuesNulls = np.isnan (artists_billboard
['age_in_billboard'])

7

8       artists_billboard.loc [np.isnan (artists_billboard
['age_in_billboard']), 'age_in_billboard'] =
age_null_random_list

9       artists_billboard ['age_in_billboard'] =
artists_billboard ['age_in_billboard']. astype (int)

10      print ("Average Age:" + str (age_avg))

11      print ("Deflected Std Age:" + str (age_std))

12      print ("Interval to assign random age:" + str (int
(age_avg - age_std)) + "a" + str (int (age_avg + age_std)))
```

Although the ideal is to have the real information , and in fact we can obtain it by searching Wikipedia (or other music websites), I wanted to show another way to be able to complete missing data while maintaining the average ages we had in our data set.

We can visualize the values that we add (in green color) in the following graph:

```
1       f1 = artists_billboard ['age_in_billboard']. values

2       f2 = artists_billboard.index

3

4       colors = ['orange', 'blue', 'green']

5

6       assign = []

7       for index, row in artists_billboard.iterrows ():

8               if (withValuesNulls [index]):

9               assign.append (colors [2]) # green

10              else:

11                      assign.append (colors [row ['top']])

12

13      plt.scatter (f1, f2, c = assign, s = 30)

14      plt.axis ([15,50,0,650])

15      plt.show ()
```

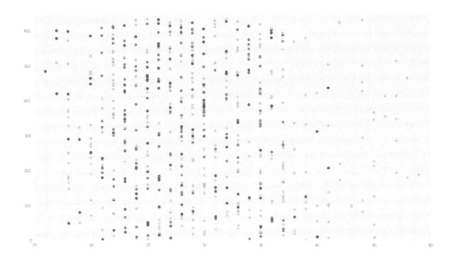

Data Mapping

We will transform several of the input data into categorical values. The ages, we separate them into: under 21, between 21 and 26, etc. song durations too, e.g., between 150 and 180 seconds, etc. For moods, I grouped those that were similar.

The Tempo that can be slow, medium or fast is mapped: 0-Fast, 1-Slow, 2-Medium (by number of songs in each tempo: the Medium has the most).

1   # Mood Mapping

2   artists_billboard ['moodEncoded'] = artists_billboard ['mood']. map ({'Energizing': 6,

3   'Empowering': 6,

4   'Cool': 5,

```
5          'Yearning': 4, # yearning, desire, craving

6          'Excited': 5, # excited

7          'Defiant': 3,

8          'Sensual': 2,

9      'Gritty': 3, # courage

10         'Sophisticated': 4,

11         'Aggressive': 4, # provocative

12         'Fiery': 4, # strong character

13         'Urgent': 3,

14         'Rowdy': 4, # loud noise

15         'Sentimental': 4,

16         'Easygoing': 1, # single

17         'Melancholy': 4,

18         'Romantic': 2,

19         'Peaceful': 1,

20         'Brooding': 4, # melancholic

21         'Upbeat': 5, # cheerful optimist

22          'Stirring': 5, # exciting

23          'Lively': 5, # animated
```

```
24                          'Other': 0, '': 0}) .astype (int)

25      # Tempo Mapping

26      artists_billboard ['tempoEncoded'] = artists_billboard
['tempo']. map ({'Fast Tempo': 0, 'Medium Tempo': 2, 'Slow
Tempo': 1, '': 0}) .astype (int)

27      # Genre Mapping

28      artists_billboard ['genreEncoded'] = artists_billboard
['genre']. map ({'Urban': 4,

29                          'Pop': 3,

30                          'Traditional': 2,

31                          'Alternative & Punk': 1,

32                          'Electronics': 1,

33                          'Rock': 1,

34                          'Soundtrack': 0,

35                          'Jazz': 0,

36                          'Other': 0, '': 0}

37                          ) .astype (int)

38      # artist_type Mapping

39      artists_billboard ['artist_typeEncoded'] = artists_billboard
['artist_type']. map ({'Female': 2, 'Male': 3, 'Mixed': 1, '': 0}) .astype
(int)
```

```
40

41

42      # Mapping age at which they reached the billboard

43      artists_billboard.loc [artists_billboard ['age_in_billboard']
<= 21, 'ageEncoded'] = 0

44      artists_billboard.loc [(artists_billboard ['age_in_billboard']>
21) & (artists_billboard ['age_en_billboard'] <= 26), 'ageEncoded']
= 1

45      artists_billboard.loc [(artists_billboard ['age_in_billboard']>
26) & (artists_billboard ['age_en_billboard'] <= 30), 'ageEncoded']
= 2

46      artists_billboard.loc [(artists_billboard ['age_in_billboard']>
30) & (artists_billboard ['age_in_billboard'] <= 40), 'ageEncoded']
= 3

47      artists_billboard.loc [artists_billboard ['age_in_billboard']>
40, 'ageEncoded'] = 4

48

49      # Mapping Song Duration

50      artists_billboard.loc [artists_billboard ['durationSeg'] <=
150, 'durationEncoded'] = 0

51      artists_billboard.loc [(artists_billboard ['durationSeg']> 150)
& (artists_billboard ['durationSeg'] <= 180), 'durationEncoded'] = 1
```

52   artists_billboard.loc [(artists_billboard ['durationSeg']> 180) & (artists_billboard ['durationSeg'] <= 210), 'durationEncoded'] = 2

53   artists_billboard.loc [(artists_billboard ['durationSeg']> 210) & (artists_billboard ['durationSeg'] <= 240), 'durationEncoded'] = 3

54   artists_billboard.loc [(artists_billboard ['durationSeg']> 240) & (artists_billboard ['durationSeg'] <= 270), 'durationEncoded'] = 4

55   artists_billboard.loc [(artists_billboard ['durationSeg']> 270) & (artists_billboard ['durationSeg'] <= 300), 'durationEncoded'] = 5

56   artists_billboard.loc [artists_billboard ['durationSeg']> 300, 'durationEncoded'] = 6

Finally we get a new data set called artists_encoded with which we have the definitive attributes to create our tree. To do this, we remove all the columns we don't need with «drop»:

1   drop_elements = ['id', 'title', 'artist', 'mood', 'tempo', 'genre', 'artist_type', 'chart_date', 'anioBirth', 'durationSeg', 'age_in_billboard']

2   artists_encoded = artists_billboard.drop (drop_elements, axis = 1)

How are the Top Left in Relation to the Mapped Data

Let's review in tables how the top = 1 are distributed in the various mapped attributes. On the sum column, the top ones will be, since being a value of 0 or 1, only those that did reach number 1 will be added.

1   artists_encoded   [['moodEncoded', 'top']].   groupby (['moodEncoded'], as_index = False) .agg (['mean', 'count', 'sum'])

	top		
	mean	count	sum
moodEncoded			
0	0.000000	1	0
1	0.000000	8	0
2	0.274194	62	17
3	0.145631	103	15
4	0.136986	146	20
5	0.294872	156	46
6	0.270440	159	43

We see most of the top 1 in moods 5 and 6 with 46 and 43 songs

1   artists_encoded [['artist_typeEncoded', 'top']]. groupby (['artist_typeEncoded'], as_index = False) .agg (['mean', 'count', 'sum'])

	top		
	mean	count	sum
artist_typeEncoded			
1	0.305263	95	29
2	0.320261	153	49
3	0.162791	387	63

Here they are quite distributed, but there is a majority in type 3: male artists

1   artists_encoded [['genreEncoded', 'top']]. groupby (['genreEncoded'], as_index = False) .agg (['mean', 'count', 'sum'])

	top		
	mean	count	sum
genreEncoded			

0	0.105263	19	2
1	0.070000	100	7
2	0.008850	113	1
3	0.319149	188	60
4	0.330233	215	71

The genres with a majority are obviously genres 3 and 4 that correspond to Urban and Pop.

1   artists_encoded [['tempoEncoded', 'top']]. groupby (['tempoEncoded'], as_index = False) .agg (['mean', 'count', 'sum'])

	top		
	mean	count	sum
tempo Encoded			
0	0.226415	53	12
1	0.246154	65	16
2	0.218569	517	113

The tempo with the most successful songs at number 1 is 2, medium tempo.

1   artists_encoded [['durationEncoded', 'top']]. groupby ([" durationEncoded '], as_index = False) .agg ([' mean ',' count ',' sum '])

	top		
	mean	count	sum
durationEncoded			
0.0	0.295775	71	21
1.0	0.333333	30	10
2.0	0.212963	108	23
3.0	0.202381	168	34
4.0	0.232143	112	26
5.0	0.145455	55	8
6.0	0.208791	91	19

They are quite distributed in relation to the length of the songs.

1   artists_encoded [['ageEncoded', 'top']]. groupby ([" Encoded age '], as_index = False) .agg ([' mean ',' count ',' sum '])

	top		
	mean	count	sum
edadEncoded			
0.0	0.257576	66	17
1.0	0.300613	163	49
2.0	0.260563	142	37
3.0	0.165899	217	36
4.0	0.042553	47	2

Age with a majority is type 1 that includes from 21 to 25 years.

We look for the depth for our decision tree

We almost have our tree. Before creating it, let's find out how many levels of depth we will assign. To do this, we will take advantage of the KFold function that will help us create several subgroups with our input data to validate and assess trees with varying levels of depth. Among them, we will choose the one with the best result.

We Create the Tree and We Tune It

To create the tree, we use the sklearn tree.DecisionTreeClasifier library because we look for a classification tree (not Regression). We configure it with the parameters:

- criterion = entropy or it could be gini, but we use categorical entries

- min_samples_split = 20 refers to the minimum number of samples that a node must have to subdivide.

- min_samples_leaf = 5 minimum quantity that a final sheet can have. If I had less, that sheet would not form and "rise" one level, its predecessor.

- class_weight = {1: 3.5} **IMPORTANT:** with this we compensate for any imbalances . In our case, as I was saying before, we have fewer labels of type top = 1 (the artists who reached number 1 in the ranking). Therefore, we assign 3.5 weight to label 1 to compensate. The value comes out of dividing the amount of top = 0 (it's 494) with the top = 1 (it's 141).

NOTE: these values assigned to the parameters were put after trial and error (many times visualizing the tree, in the next step and going back to this).

1   cv = KFold (n_splits = 10) # Desired number of "folds" that we will do

```
2          accuracies = list ()

3          max_attributes = len (list (artists_encoded))

4          depth_range = range (1, max_attributes + 1)

5

6          # We will test the depth of 1 to number of attributes +1

7          for depth in depth_range:

8                   fold_accuracy = []

9                   tree_model = tree.DecisionTreeClassifier (criterion
= 'entropy',

10                                       min_samples_split = 20,

11                                       min_samples_leaf = 5,

12                                       max_depth = depth,

13                                       class_weight = {1: 3.5})

14                   for train_fold, valid_fold in cv.split
(artists_encoded):

15                           f_train = artists_encoded.loc [train_fold]

16                           f_valid = artists_encoded.loc [valid_fold]

17

18                           model = tree_model.fit (X = f_train.drop
(['top'], axis = 1),

19                                              y = f_train ["top"])

20                           valid_acc = model.score (X = f_valid.drop
(['top'], axis = 1),
```

```
21          y = f_valid ["top"]) # calculate the precision with the
validation segment

22                          fold_accuracy.append (valid_acc)

23

24              avg = sum (fold_accuracy) / len (fold_accuracy)

25              accuracies.append (avg)

26

27      # We show the results obtained

28      df = pd.DataFrame ({"Max Depth": depth_range, "Average
Accuracy": accuracies})

29      df = df [["Max Depth", "Average Accuracy"]]

30      print (df.to_string (index = False))
```

Max Depth	Average Accuraccy
1	0.556101
2	0.556126
3	0.564038
4	0.648859
5	0.617386
6	0.614236
7	0.625124

We can see that in 4 levels of splits we have the highest score, with almost 65%.

Now we can only create and visualize our tree of 4 levels of depth.

Decision Tree Display

We assign the input data and the parameters that we previously configured with 4 levels of depth. We will use the export_graphviz function to create a .dot extension file that we will then convert into a png graphic to visualize the tree.

```
1      # Create training arrays and labels that indicate
whether it reached top or not

2      y_train = artists_encoded ['top']

3      x_train = artists_encoded.drop (['top'], axis = 1)
.values

4

5      # Create Decision Tree with depth = 4

6      decision_tree = tree.DecisionTreeClassifier
(criterion = 'entropy',

7                          min_samples_split = 20,

8                          min_samples_leaf = 5,

9                          max_depth = 4,

10                          class_weight = {1: 3.5})

11     decision_tree.fit (x_train, y_train)
```

```
12      # export the model to a .dot file

13      with open (r "tree1.dot", 'w') as f:

14      f = tree.export_graphviz (decision_tree,

15                      out_file = f,

16                      max_depth = 7,

17                      impurity = True,

18      feature_names = list (artists_encoded.drop (['top'],
axis = 1)),

19                          class_names = ['No', 'N1 Billboard'],

20                          rounded = True,

21                          filled = True)

22

23

24      # Convert the .dot file to png to view

25      check_call (['dot', '- Tpng', r'tree1.dot ',' - o ',
r'tree1.png'])

26      PImage ("tree1.png")
```

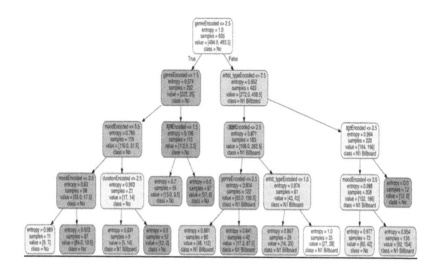

At last, our precious tree appears on the screen! Now we will have to look and see if we can improve it (for example, tuning the input parameters).

Conclusions and Analysis of the Tree

In the graph we see, a root node that makes the first subdivision by gender and the outputs go to the left for True that is less than 2.5, that is, the genera 0, 1 and 2 (they were the least top = 1 had) and right in False go genres 3 and 4 that was Pop and Urban with lots of top Billboard users.

In the second level, we see that the quantity of samples (samples) is distributed in 232 and 403, respectively.

As we lower the level, we will see that the entropy values are closer to 1 when the node has more samples top = 1 (blue) and approach 0 when there are a majority of samples Top = 0 (orange).

At various levels, we will see divisions by type of artist, age, duration, and mood. We also see some orange leaves that end before reaching the last level: this is because they reach a zero entropy level, or because they are left with a smaller quantity of samples than our minimum allowed to split (20).

Let's see what the accuracy achieved by our tree was:

```
1       acc_decision_tree = round (decision_tree.score
(x_train, y_train) * 100, 2)

2       print (acc_decision_tree)
```

It gives us a value of 64.88%. We notice that almost all the final leaves of the tree have mixed samples, especially in the output, to classify the top = 1. This causes the score to be reduced.

Let's test our algorithm

Prediction of Songs to Billboard 100

We are going to test our tree with 2 artists who entered billboard 100 in 2017: Camila Cabello who reached number 1 with the Havana Song and Imagine Dragons with her song Believer that reached a 42nd position but did not reach the top.

```
1       #preach artist CAMILA CABELLO featuring
YOUNG THUG

2       # with his song Havana came to number 1 Billboard
US in 2017

3
```

```
4      x_test = pd.DataFrame (columns = ('top',
'moodEncoded', 'tempoEncoded', 'genreEncoded',
'artist_typeEncoded', 'ageEncoded', 'durationEncoded'))

6      x_test.loc [0] = (1,5,2,4,1,0,3)

7      y_pred = decision_tree.predict (x_test.drop (['top'],
axis = 1))

print ("Prediction:" + str (y_pred))

8      y_proba = decision_tree.predict_proba (x_test.drop
(['top'], axis = 1))

9      print ("Probability of Success:" + str (round
(y_proba [0] [y_pred] * 100, 2)) + "%")
```

It gives us that Havana will reach the top 1 with a probability of 83%. Nothing bad...

```
1      #preach artist Imagine Dragons

2      # with his song Believer reached 42nd Billboard US
in 2017

3

4      x_test = pd.DataFrame (columns = ('top',
'moodEncoded', 'tempoEncoded', 'genreEncoded',
'artist_typeEncoded', 'ageEncoded', 'durationEncoded'))

5      x_test.loc [0] = (0,4,2,1,3,2,3)

6      y_pred = decision_tree.predict (x_test.drop (['top'],
axis = 1))
```

7   print ("Prediction:" + str (y_pred))

8   y_proba = decision_tree.predict_proba (x_test.drop (['top'], axis = 1))

9   print ("Probability of Success:" + str (round (y_proba [0] [y_pred] * 100, 2)) + "%")

It gives us that the Imagine Dragons song will NOT arrive with a certainty of 88%. Another success.

Let's see the paths taken by each of the songs:

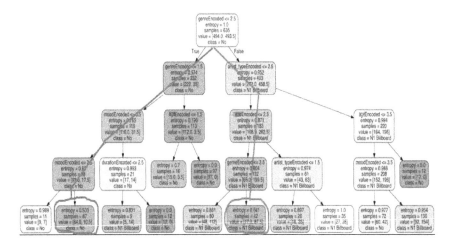

Here we see the roads taken by Havana in Pink, which reached number 1 and the road through Believer (in Red) that did not arrive.

Summary of the Chapter

Well, we had a long way to create and generate our tree. We have reviewed the input data, we have processed it, and we pass it to categorical values and generate the tree. We have put it to the test to validate it.

Obtaining a score of less than 65% in the tree is not a very high value, but let's keep in mind that we set ourselves a somewhat tricky task: to be able to predict Billboard number 1 and with such a small sample size (635 records) and unbalanced. They already want record labels to be able to do it.

SIX

Linear Regression with Python

What is the Linear Regression?

The linear regression is an algorithm of supervised learning used in Machine Learning and statistics. In its simplest version, what we will do is "draw a line" that will indicate the trend of a continuous data set (if they were discrete, we would use Logistic Regression).

In statistics, linear regression is an approximation to model the relationship between a dependent scalar variable «and» and one or more explanatory variables named with «X.»

Let's quickly remember the formula of the line:

$$Y = mX + b$$

Where Y is the result, X is the variable, m the slope (or coefficient) of the line and b the constant or also known as the "cut-off point with the Y-axis" on the graph (when X = 0)

How Does the Linear Regression Algorithm Work in Machine Learning?

Recall that the Supervised Machine Learning algorithms, learn by themselves and - in this case - to automatically get that "straight" that we look for with the prediction trend. Achieving this requires that the error is measured for the entry points and the actual "Y" value. The algorithm should minimize the cost of a quadratic error function, and those coefficients will correspond to the optimal line. There are various methods to reduce cost. The most common is to use a vector version and the so-called Normal Equation that will give us a direct result.

NOTE: *When I speak of "straight," it is in the particular case of simple linear regression. If there were more variables, the term must be generalized.*

Let's Do a Practical Exercise

In this example, we will load an input .csv file obtained by webscraping that contains various URLs from articles about Machine Learning from some significant sites such as Techcrunch or KDnuggets and as input features - the columns - we will have:

- Title: Article Title

- url: the path to the article

- Word count: the number of words in the article,

- # of Links: the external links it contains,

- # of comments: number of comments,

- # Images & videos: the sum of images (or videos),

- Elapsed days: the number of days elapsed (at the time of creating the file)

- # Shares: our output column that will be the "number of times the article was shared."

From the characteristics of a machine learning article, we will try to predict how many times it will be shared in Social Networks.

We will make a first simple linear regression prediction -with a single predictor variable- to be able to graph in 2 dimensions (X and Y axes) and then an example of Multiple Linear regression, in which we will use three dimensions (X, Y, Z) and predictions.

NOTE: *The .csv file contains half of the real data, and another half generated them randomly, so the predictions we will get will not be real.*

Requirements to do the Exercise

To perform this exercise, I suggest you create a Jupyter notebook with Python code and the SkLearn library widely used in Data Science. I also recommend using the Anaconda suite. You can read again chapter 2, where I show step by step how to install the development environment.

Simple Linear Regression in Python (with one variable)

Here we need to go with our notebook!

Let's start by importing the libraries, we will use:

```
1       Let'# Imports needed

2       import numpy as np

3       import pandas as pd

4       import seaborn as sb

5       import matplotlib.pyplot as plt

6       % matplotlib inline

7       from mpl_toolkits.mplot3d import Axes3D

8       from matplotlib import cm

9       plt.rcParams ['figure.figsize'] = (16, 9)

10      plt.style.use ('ggplot')

11      from sklearn import linear_model

12      from sklearn.metrics import mean_squared_error, r2_scores
```

Now we need to read the csv file and load it as a Pandas dataset. And we will see its size.

```
1       #We load the input data

2       data = pd.read_csv ("./ articles_ml.csv")

3       # let's see how many dimensions and records it contains

4       data.shape
```

It returns us (161.8)

Let's look at those first rows:

1   # there are 161 records with 8 columns. Let's see the first records

2   data.head ()

	Title	url	Word count	# of Links	# of comments	# Images video	Elapsed days	# Shares
0	What is Machine Learning and how do we use it ...	https://biog.signals.network/what-is-machine-I...	1888	1	2.0	2	34	200000
1	10 Companies Using Machine Learning in Cool Ways	NaN	1742	9	NaN	9	5	25000
2	How Artificial Intelligence Is Revolutionizing...	NaN	962	6	0.0	1	10	42000
3	Dbrain and the Blockchain of Artificial Intell...	NaN	1221	3	NaN	2	68	200000
4	Nasa finds entire solar system filled with eig...	NaN	2039	1	104.0	4	131	200000

You see some fields with NaN values (null), for example, some URLs or in comments.

Let's look at some basic statistics of our input data:

1   # Now let's see some statistics of our data

2   data.describe ()

	Word count	# of Links	# of comments	# Images video	Elapsed days	# Shares
count	161.000000	161.000000	129.000000	161.000000	161.000000	161.000000
mean	1808.260870	9.739130	8.782946	3.670807	98.124224	27948.347826
std	1141.919385	47.271625	13.142822	3.418290	114.337535	43408.006839
min	250.000000	0.000000	0.000000	1.000000	1.000000	0.000000
25%	990.000000	3.000000	2.000000	1.000000	31.000000	2800.000000
50%	1674.000000	5.000000	6.000000	3.000000	62.000000	16458.000000
75%	2369.000000	7.000000	12.000000	5.000000	124.000000	35691.000000
max	8401.000000	600.000000	104.000000	22.000000	1002.000000	350000.000000

Here we see that the average words in the articles are 1808. The shortest article has 250 words and the most extensive 8401. We will try to see with our linear relationship if there is a correlation between the number of words in the text and the number of Shares obtained.

We make a general visualization of the input data:

```
1      # We quickly visualize the input characteristics

2      data.drop (['Title', 'url', 'Elapsed days'], 1) .hist ()

3      plt.show ()
```

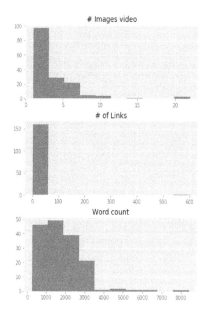
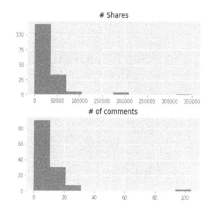

In these graphs, we see among which values the majority of records are concentrated.

We are going to filter the word quantity data to keep the records with less than 3500 words and also with those with a number of shares less than 80,000. We will reward you by painting the dots with less than 1808 words (the average) in blue and those with more in orange.

```
1       # We will CUT the data in the area where the points are
most concentrated

2       # this is on the X axis: between 0 and 3,500

3       # and on the Y axis: between 0 and 80,000

4       filtered_data = data [(data ['Word count'] <= 3500) & (data
['# Shares'] <= 80000)]

5

6       colors = ['orange', 'blue']

7       sizes = [30,60]

8

9       f1 = filtered_data ['Word count']. values

10      f2 = filtered_data ['# Shares']. values

11

12      # We are going to paint the points below and above the
average number of words in colors

13      assign = []

14      for index, row in filtered_data.iterrows ():

15              if (row ['Word count']> 1808):

16                      assign.append (colors [0])
```

```
17            else:
18                    assign.append (colors [1])
19
20      plt.scatter (f1, f2, c = assign, s = sizes [0])
21      plt.show ()
```

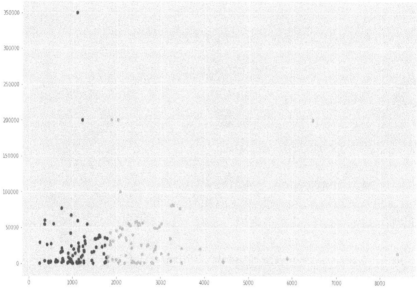

Linear Regression with Python and SKLearn

We will create our input data for the moment only Word Count and as tags the # Shares. We create the Linear Regression object and make it "fit" (train) with the fit () method. Finally we print the coefficients and scores obtained.

```python
1       # We assign our input variable X for training and the Y
labels.

2       dataX = filtered_data [["Word count"]]

3       X_train = np.array (dataX)

4       y_train = filtered_data ['# Shares']. values

5

6       # We create the Linear Regression object

7       regr = linear_model.LinearRegression ()

8

9       # We train our model

10      regr.fit (X_train, y_train)

11

12      # We make predictions that ultimately a line (in this case,
being 2D)

13      y_pred = regr.predict (X_train)

14

15      # Let's see the coefficients obtained, In our case, they will
be the Tangent

16      print ('Coefficients: \ n', regr.coef_)

17      # This is the value where the Y axis cuts (at X = 0)
```

18   print ('Independent term: \ n', regr.intercept_)

19   # Medium Square Error

20   print ("Mean squared error:% .2f"% mean_squared_error (y_train, y_pred))

21   # Variance score. The best score is a 1.0

22   print ('Variance score:% .2f% r2_score (y_train, y_pred))

<

p style = »padding-left: 30px;»> Coefficients: [5.69765366]

Independent term: 11200.303223074163

Mean squared error: 372888728.34

Variance score: 0.06

From the equation of the line $y = mX + b$ our slope «m» is the coefficient 5.69 and the independent term «b» is 11200. We have a huge mean square error ... so in reality this model will not be very good. But we are learning to use it, which is what matters to us now. This is also reflected in the Variance score that should be close to 1.0.

Let's Visualize the Straight

Let's see the line we obtained:

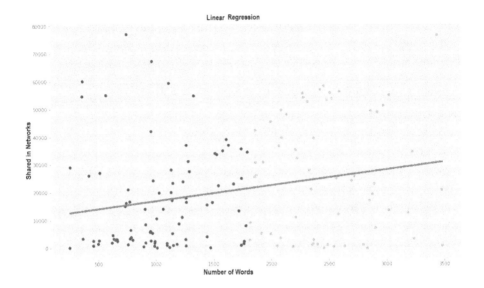

Simple Linear Regression Prediction

We will try to test our algorithm, assuming we would like to predict how many "share" you will get an article on ML of 2000 words.

1   # Let's check:

2   # I want to predict how many "Shares" I will get for an article with 2,000 words,

3   # according to our model, we do:

4   y_Two thousand = regr.predict ([[2000]])

5   print (int (y_Dosmil))

It returns a prediction of 22595 "Shares" for a 2000-word article (I would like to!).

134

Multiple Linear Regression in Python (or "Regression with Multiple Variables")

We will extend the exercise using more than one input variable for the model. This gives more power to the Machine Learning algorithm because, in this way, we can obtain more complex predictions.

Our "equation of the Straight" now becomes:

$$Y = b + m1 \ X1 + m2 \ X2 + \ldots + m \ (n) \ X \ (n)$$

and stop being a straight line)

In our case, we will use 2 «predictive variables» to be able to graph in 3D, but remember that for better predictions, we can use more than 2 inputs and dispense with the graph.

Our first variable will remain the number of words and the second variable will be the sum of 3 input columns: the number of links, comments and number of images. We are going to program!

```
1        #We will try to improve the Model, with one more
         dimension:

2        # To be able to graph in 3D, we will make a new
         variable that will be the sum of the links, comments and
         images

3        sum = (filtered_data ["# of Links"] + filtered_data
         ['# of comments']. fillna (0) + filtered_data ['# Images
         video'])

4

5        dataX2 = pd.DataFrame ()
```

6   dataX2 ["Word count"] = filtered_data ["Word count"]

7   dataX2 ["sum"] = sum

8   XY_train = np.array (dataX2)

9   z_train = filtered_data ['# Shares']. Values

Note: *it would have been better to apply PCA for size reduction , maintaining the most important information of all.*

We already have our two input variables in XY_train, and our output variable goes from being «Y» to being the «Z» axis.

We create a new Linear Regression object with SKLearn, but this time, it will have the two dimensions to train: those contained in XY_train. As before, we print the coefficients and scores obtained:

1   # We create a new Linear Regression object

2   regr2 = linear_model.LinearRegression ()

3

4   # We train the model, this time, with two dimensions

5   # we will get two coefficients, to graph a plane

6   regr2.fit (XY_train, z_train)

7   # We make the prediction with which we will have points on the plane found

```
8       z_pred = regr2.predict (XY_train)

9

10      # The coefficients

11      print ('Coefficients: \ n', regr2.coef_)

12      # Mean square error

13      print ("Mean squared error:% .2f"%
mean_squared_error (z_train, z_pred))

14      # We evaluate the variance score (1.0 being the best
possible)

15      print ('Variance score:% .2f% r2_score (z_train,
z_pred))
```

<

p style = »padding-left: 30px;»> Coefficients: [6.63216324 -
483.40753769]

Mean squared error: 352122816.48

Variance score: 0.11

As we see, we obtain 2 coefficients (each corresponding to our 2 predictive variables), because now what we graph will not be a line if not, a plane in 3 Dimensions.

The error obtained is still significant, although somewhat better than the previous one, and the variance score improves almost double the previous one (although it is still terrible, far from 1).

Display a Plane in 3 Dimensions in Python

We will graph our points of the input characteristics in blue and the points projected on the plane in red. Recall that in this graph, the Z axis corresponds to the "height" and represents the number of Shares we will obtain.

```
1       fig = plt.figure ()

2       ax = Axes3D (fig)

3

4       # We create a mesh, on which we will graph the plane

5       xx, yy = np.meshgrid (np.linspace (0, 3500, num =
10), np.linspace (0, 60, num = 10))

6

7       # we calculate the values of the plane for the points x
and y

8       newX = (regr2.coef_ [0] * xx)

9       newY = (regr2.coef_ [1] * yy)

10

11      # we calculate the corresponding values for z. We
must add the interception point

12      z = (newX + newY + regr2.intercept_)

13
```

```
14      # We plot the plane

15      ax.plot_surface (xx, yy, z, alpha = 0.2, cmap = 'hot')

16

17      # We plot the points in blue in 3D

18      ax.scatter (XY_train [:, 0], XY_train [:, 1], z_train, c
= 'blue', s = 30)

19

20      # We plot in red, the points that

21      ax.scatter (XY_train [:, 0], XY_train [:, 1], z_pred, c
= 'red', s = 40)

22

23      # with this we place the "camera" with which we
visualize

24      ax.view_init (elev = 30., azim = 65)

25

26      ax.set_xlabel ('Number of Words')

27      ax.set_ylabel ('Number of Links, Comments and
Images')

28      ax.set_zlabel ('Shared in Networks')

29      ax.set_title ('Linear Regression with Multiple
Variables')
```

We can rotate the plot to appreciate the plane from different angles by changing the value of the parameter azim in view_init with numbers from 0 to 360.

Prediction with the Multiple Variables model

Let's see now, what prediction we will have for a 2000 word article, with ten links, four comments and six images.

```
1       # If I want to predict how many "Shares" I will get
for an article with:

2       # 2000 words and with links: 10, comments: 4,
images: 6

3       # according to our model, we do:

4

5       z_Dosmil = regr2.predict ([[2000, 10 + 4 + 6]])

6       print (int (z_Dosmil))
```

This prediction gives us 20518 and is probably a little better than our previous prediction with one variable.

Summary of the Chapter and Improvement of our Model

We have seen how to use SKLearn in Python to create Linear Regression models with one or multiple variables. In our exercise, we did not have great confidence in the predictions. For example, in our first model, with 2000 words, it predicts that we can have 22595, but the margin of error making the root of the mean quartic error is less than 19310. That is to say that writing an article of 2000 words

the same we have 3285 Shares than 41905. In this case, we use this model to learn how to use it, and it will have to be seen in other instances where it does give us accurate predictions.

To improve our model, we should use more dimensions and find better input data.

Attention: it is also possible that there is never any relationship between our input variables and the success in Shares of an article with which we can never predict with the certainty of this output. This was an experiment!

CHAPTER
SEVEN

The Artificial Neural Networks & Deep Learning

Architectures and Applications of the Most Used Neural Networks

Neural Networks are modeled as a set of neurons connected as an acyclic graph. What does this mean in practice? This means that the outputs (outputs) of some neurons are the inputs (inputs) from other neurons.

The most commonly encountered Neural Networks, there are those arranged in layers (layers) different, and each layer containing a set of neurons. The most commonly encountered layer type is that of the fully-connected layer type. In this, neurons between two adjacent layers connect two by two.

This type of architecture is also known as Neural Network Feedforward, and it is only allowed to a neuron layer l_i connect to a neuron of the layer $L_i + 1$, as shown in the figure below.

We will review the various structures invented, improved, and used throughout history to create neural networks and get the most out of

Deep Learning to solve all kinds of regression and classification problems.

The purpose of this post is actually to implement an implementation through the Keras library. For a more complete and detailed introduction to the subject, as well as the basics of deep learning.

Evolution of Neural Networks in Computer Science

We will review the following networks/architectures:

- 1958 - Perceptron

- 1965 - Multilayer Perceptron

- 1980's

    o Sigmoidal Neurons

    o Feedforward networks

    o Backpropagation

- 1989 - Convolutional neural networks (CNN) / Recurrent neural networks (RNN)

- 1997 - Long short term memory (LSTM)

- 2006 - Deep Belief Networks (DBN): Deep Learning is Born

    o Restricted Boltzmann Machine

    o Encoder / Decoder = Auto-encoder

- 2014 - Generative Adversarial Networks (GAN)

While this list is not exhaustive and does not cover all the models created since the 1950s, I have compiled what were - in my opinion - the most important networks and technologies developed to reach the point where we are today: Deep Learning.

The Beginning of Everything: the Artificial Neuron

1958 – Perceptron

Between the 1950s and 1960s, scientist Frank Rosenblatt, inspired by the work of Warren McCulloch and Walter Pitts, created the Perceptron, the unit from which artificial neural networks would be born and enhanced.

A perceptron takes several binary inputs x1, x2, etc. and produces only one binary output. To calculate the output, Rosenblatt introduces the concept of «weights» w1, w2, etc., a real number that expresses the importance of the respective input with the output. The output of the neuron will be 1 or 0 if the sum of the multiplication of weights by inputs is greater or less than a certain threshold.

Its main uses are simple binary decisions, or to create logical functions such as OR, AND.

1965 - Multilayer Perceptron

As you can imagine, the perceptron multilayer is an "amplification" of the perception of a single neuron to more than one. Also, the concept of input, hidden, and output layers appear. But with binary input and output values. Let us not forget that both the value of the weights and the threshold value of each neuron were assigned manually by the scientist. The more perceptrons in the layers, the harder to get the weights to get desired outputs.

The 1980s: Machine Learning

Sigmoid Neurons

To make neuron networks learn alone, it was necessary to introduce a new type of neuron. The so-called Sigmoid Neurons are similar to the perceptron but allow the inputs, instead of being zeroes or ones, to have real values such as 0.5 or 0.377 or whatever. There are also "bias" neurons that always add up to 1 in the various layers to solve certain situations. Now the outputs instead of being 0 or 1, will be d (w. X + b) where d will be the sigmoid function defined as d $(z) = 1 / (1 + e^{-z})$. This is the first activation function!

With this new formula, small alterations in values of the weights (deltas) can produce minor modifications in the output. Therefore, we can gradually adjust the weights of the connections and obtain the desired outputs.

Feedforward Networks

Networks are thus called in that the outputs of one layer are used as inputs in the next layer. This means that there are no "backward" loops. It always "feeds" on values forward. There are networks that we will see later in which there are those loops (Recurrent Neural Networks).

Also, there is the concept of "fully connected Feedforward Networks," and it refers to all input neurons, are connected to all neurons of the next layer.

1986 - Backpropagation

Thanks to the backpropagation algorithm, it was possible to train multilayer neural networks in a supervised manner. When calculating the error obtained at the output and propagating to the previous layers, small adjustments (minimizing cost) are made in each iteration to ensure that the network learns so that the network can, for example, classify the inputs correctly.

1989 - Convolutional Neural Network

A convolutional neural network (with the acronyms CNNs or ConvNets) is a specific case of Deep Learning neural networks, which were already used in the late 90s but which in recent years have become popular when getting impressive results in image recognition, impacting deeply in the area of computer vision.

The convolutional neural networks are very similar to the neural networks of the previous chapter: they are formed by neurons that have parameters in the form of weights and biases that can be learned. But a differential feature of CNNs is that they make the explicit assumption that entries are images, which allows us to encode certain properties in the architecture to recognize specific elements in the images.

To get an intuitive idea of how these neural networks work, let's think about how we recognize things. For example, if we see a face, we recognize it because it has ears, eyes, nose, hair, etc. So, to decide if something is a face, we do it as if we had some mental boxes of verification of the characteristics that we are marking.

Sometimes a face may not have an ear because the hair covers it, but we also classify it with a certain probability as a face because we see the eyes, nose, and mouth. We can see it as a classifier equivalent to that presented in Chapter 2, which predicts a probability that the input image is expensive or not expensive.

But in reality, we must first know what an ear or nose is like to know if they are in an image; that is, we must previously identify lines, borders, textures, or shapes that are similar to those contained in the ears or noses that we have seen before. And this is what the layers of a convolutional neural network are entrusted to do.

1997 Long Short Term Memory / Recurrent Neural Network

Recurrent Neural Networks (RNN in English), are currently the most powerful technology we have in supervised learning, and now we are going to explain why, because this algorithm is so advanced and so powerful.

As we had spoken before, the concept on which deep learning is based, is to try to imitate the human brain, and it would be interesting to associate the Recurring Neural Networks with some part of the human brain, and the part with which we will associate it will be the Temporal lobe, which is responsible for long-term memory.

The temporal lobe ensures that the information is not lost over time. For example, imagine tomorrow not being able to remember this article, just remember it today that you read it. Then the Recurring Neural Networks could be compared with the temporal lobe.

Deep Learning is Achieved

2006 - Deep Belief Networks (DBN)

Before the NBD in 2006, models with "depth" (tens or hundreds of layers) were considered too difficult to train (even with backpropagation), and the use of artificial neural networks was stagnant. With the creation of a DBN that achieved a better result in the MNIST, the enthusiasm in being able to achieve deep learning in neural networks was returned.

Nowadays, the DBNs are not used much, but they were a significant milestone in the history of the development of deep learning and allowed to continue the exploration to improve the existing networks CNN, LSTM, etc.

The Deep Belief Networks, showed that using random weights when initializing networks is a bad idea: for example, when using Backpropagation with Gradient Descent, many times it fell to local lows, without optimizing the weights. It will be better to use an intelligent weight allocation utilizing a pre-training of the network layers.

It is based on the use of Restricted Boltzmann Machines and Autoencoders to pre-train the network in an unsupervised manner. Eye! After pre-training and assigning those initial weights, we must train the network on a regular, supervised basis (for example, with backpropagation).

It is believed that this pre-training is one of the causes of the significant improvement in the neural networks and allow deep learning: because to assign the values, it is evaluated layer by layer, one by one, and does not "suffer" from a particular bias that causes backpropagation, when training all layers simultaneously.

2014 - Generative Adversarial Networks

These networks can learn to create samples, similar to the data we feed them with Antagonistic Generative Networks, or Generative Adversarial Networks in English (GAN), which is a powerful class of neural networks. One could say that they have become one of the pillars of the recent "boom" of the so-called Artificial Intelligence. Ian Goodfellow presented them in 2014, and since then, they have allowed a significant advance in the field of machine learning without supervision.

GANs are one of the most exciting tools of AI, but their implementation requires a specific domain, especially in numerical methods. The GANs primarily consists of an algorithm based on a system of two neural networks - the Generator and the Discriminator - that compete with each other.

Its main applications are the generation of realistic images, but also to improve existing images, or generate texts (captions) in images, or generate texts following a specific style and even development of molecules for the pharmaceutical industry.

Deep Learning and Neural Networks -Without Code

In this section, I will try to explain what the Deep Learning or Learning Deep used in Machine Learning describing its basic components.

I assume that as an advanced reader, you already know the definition of Machine Learning and its main applications in the real world and the landscape of algorithms used most frequently. We will focus on Deep Learning, applying Artificial Neural Networks.

How Does Deep Learning Work?

Deep Learning is a method of Machine Learning that allows us to train an Artificial Intelligence to obtain a prediction given a set of inputs. This intelligence will achieve a level of cognition by hierarchies. You can use Learning Supervised or Unsupervised.

I will explain how Deep Learning works through a hypothetical example of prediction about who will win the next World Cup. We will use supervised learning through algorithms of Artificial Neural Networks.

To achieve the predictions of football matches, we will use the following entries as an example:

- Number of Matches Won
- Number of tied matches
- Number of Lost Matches
- Number of Goals in Favor
- Number of Goals Against

«Winning Streak» of the team (max. Number of games won in a row over the total played)

And we could have many more entries, for example, the average score of the team players, or the score given by FIFA to the team. As in each match, we have two rivals; we will have to enter this six entry data for each team, that is, six entries from team one and another six from team two, giving a total of 12 entries.

The prediction will be the result of the match: Home, Draw, or Away.

We Create a Neural Network

In this section, you will learn how to implement Multilayer Neural Networks using Python and the Deep Learning Keras library, one of the most popular today.

Keras is a library of Neural Networks, capable of running TensorFlow (not just), and was developed to make prototyping easy and fast.

Multilayered Neural Networks are those in which neurons are structured in two or more layers (layer) processing (as there are at least one layer input and one layer output).

Implementing a complete Neural Networks architecture from scratch is a Herculean task that requires a more robust understanding of Programming, Linear Algebra, and Statistics - not to mention that the computational performance of your implementation will hardly beat the performance of public libraries in the community.

To show that with a few lines of code, it is possible to implement a simple network, let's take the well-known MNIST classification problem and see how our algorithm performs when submitted to this 70,000 image dataset!

What is MNIST

MNIST is a data set that contains thousands of handwritten images from digits 0-9. The challenge with this dataset is, given any image, to apply the corresponding label (correctly classify the image). MNIST is so widely studied and used by the community that it acts as a benchmark for comparing different image recognition algorithms.

The complete dataset consists of 70,000 images, each of 28 X 28 pixels in size. The figure above shows some random copies of the dataset for each of the possible digits. It is noteworthy that the images are already normalized and centralized.

Since images are grayscale, i.e., have only one channel, the value for each pixel in the images should vary within the range [0, 255].

NIST in Python

Often used, the MNIST dataset is already available inside the library scikit-learn and can be imported directly by Python com fetch_mldata("MNIST Original").

To illustrate how to import full MNIST and extract some basic information, let's run the code below:

```
1      #import the required libraries

2      from sklearn.datasets import fetch_mldata

3      import matplotlib.pyplot as plt

4      import numpy as np

5
```

```
6        #import the MNIST dataset

7        dataset = fetch_mldata ("Original MNIST")

8        (data, labels) = (dataset.data, dataset.target)

9

10       # Display some MNIST dataset information

11       print ("[INFO] Number of images: {}". format
(data.shape [0]))

12       print ("[INFO] Pixels per image: {}". format
(data.shape [1]))

13

14       # choose a random dataset index and display

15       # the corresponding image and label

16       np.random.seed (17)

17       randomIndex = np.random.randint (0, data.shape
[0])

18       print ("[INFO] Random MNIST image with label '{:
.0f}':". format (labels [randomIndex]))

19       plt.imshow (data [randomIndex] .reshape ((28,28)),
cmap = "Grays")

20       plt.show ()
```

[INFO] Number of Images: 70000
[INFO] Pixels per image: 784
[INFO] MNIST random image with label ' 4 ' :

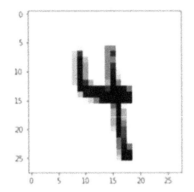

Above, we can see that the array containing the images has 70,000 rows (one row for each image) and 784 columns (all pixels of the 28 x 28 image). We can also see one of the randomly chosen images. In the case of this digit, our algorithm would have been successful if it could correctly classify the digit as '4'.

Implementing our Neural Network with Python + Keras

Having made a brief introduction about Neural Networks, we will implement a Feedforward Neural Network for the MNIST classification problem.

Create a new file in your favorite IDE, named it rede_neural_keras.py, and follow the code steps below.

```
1    #import the required packages

2    from sklearn.datasets import fetch_mldata

3    from sklearn.model_selection import train_test_split

4    from sklearn.metrics import classification_report
```

```
5      from sklearn.preprocessing import LabelBinarizer

6      from keras.models import Sequential

7      from keras.layers.core import Dense

8      from keras.optimizers import SGD

9      import numpy as np

10     import matplotlib.pyplot as plt
```

Above, we import all packages needed to create a simple Neural Network with the Keras library. If you have had an error trying to import packages, or do not have a dedicated Python virtual environment for working with Deep Learning / Computer Vision, I recommend looking for a tutorial based on your Operating System.

```
1      #import MNIST

2      print ("[INFO] importing MNIST ...")

3      dataset = fetch_mldata ("Original MNIST")

4

5      # normalize all pixels so that the values are

6      # at intervalor [0, 1.0]

7      data = dataset.data.astype ("float") / 255.0

8      labels = dataset.target
```

After importing the image set, I will split it between training set (75%) and test set (25%), a practice well known in the Data Science universe. But beware! The training and testing set MUST be INDEPENDENT, to avoid various problems, including overfitting.

Although it sounds complicated, it can be done with just one line of code, because thanks to the scikit-learn library, it can be quickly done with the method train_test_split.

In this step of preparing our data, we will also need to convert the labels - which are represented by integers - to the binary vector format. To exemplify what a binary vector is, see the example below, which indicates the label '4'.

4 = [0.0,0,0,1,0,0,0,0,0]

In this vector, the value 1 is assigned to the index corresponding to the label and the value 0 to the others. This operation, known as one-hot encoding, can also be easily done with the class LabelBinarizer.

```
1       # split dataset between train (75%) and test (25%)

2       (trainX, testX, trainY, testY) = train_test_split (date,
dataset.target)

3

4       # convert integer labels to vectors

5       lb = LabelBinarizer ()

6       trainY = lb.fit_transform (trainY)

7       testY = lb.transform (testY)
```

Ready! With the dataset imported and processed correctly, we can finally define the architecture of our Neural Network with Keras.

Arbitrarily, I defined that the Neural Network will have four layers:

- Our first layer (l_0) receive as input values for each pixel of the images. That is, as each image has a length of 28 x 28 pixels, l_0 will have 784 neurons.

- The hidden layers l_1 and l_2 will have arbitrarily 128 and 64 neurons.

- Finally, the last layer L_3, have the amount corresponding to the amount neurons classes that our own classification problem: 10 (reminiscent, 10 digits are possible).

```
1       # define Neural Network architecture using Keras

2       # 784 (input) =&gt; 128 (hidden) =&gt; 64 (hidden)
=&gt; 10 (output)

3       model = Sequential ()

4       model.add (Dense (128, input_shape = (784,),
activation = "sigmoid"))

5       model.add (Dense (64, activation = "sigmoid"))

6       model.add (Dense (10, activation = "softmax"))
```

Within the concept of feedforward architecture, our Neural Network is instantiated by the class Sequential, meaning that each layer will be "stacked" on top of another, with the output of one being the input of the next. In our example, all layers are the fully-connected layer.

The hidden layers will be activated by the function sigmoid, which takes the actual values of the neurons as input and throws them within the range [0, 1]. For the last layer, as this has to reflect the probabilities for each of the possible classes, the function will be used softmax.

To train our model, I will use the most important algorithm for Neural Networks: Stochastic Gradient Descent (SGD). I want to make a dedicated post about SGD in the future (math + code), so important! But for now, let's use the ready algorithm from our libraries.

The SGD learning rate will be 0.01, and the loss function will be a categorical_crossentropy since the number of output classes is greater than two.

```
1      # train the model using SGD (Stochastic Gradient
Descent)

2      print ("[INFO] training the neural network ...")

3      model.compile (optimizer = SGD (0.01), loss =
"categorical_crossentropy",

4                              metrics = ["accuracy"])

5      H = model.fit (trainX, trainY, batch_size = 128,
epochs = 10, verbose = 2,

6                      validation_data = (testX, testY))
```

Calling a model.fit, then begins the training of the neural network. After a time-varying according to your machine, the weights of each node are optimized, and the network can be considered as trained.

To evaluate the performance of the algorithm, we call the method model.predict to generate predictions on the top of the test dataset. The challenge of the model is to forecast the 17,500 images that make up the test suite by assigning a label of 0-9 to each:

```
1       # evaluate the Neural Network
2       print ("[INFO] evaluating the neural network ...")
3       predictions = model.predict (testX, batch_size = 128)
4       print (classification_report (testY.argmax (axis = 1),
predictions.argmax (axis = 1)))
```

Finally, after the performance report obtained, we will want to plot accuracy and loss over the iterations. Visually analyzing allows us to identify overfitting situations, for example:

```
1       # plot loss and accuracy for 'train' and 'test' datasets
2       plt.style.use ("ggplot")
3       plt.figure ()
4       plt.plot (np.arange (0.100), H.history ["loss"], label
= "train_loss")
5       plt.plot (np.arange (0.100), H.history ["val_loss"],
label = "val_loss")
6       plt.plot (np.arange (0.100), H.history ["acc"], label =
"train_acc")
7       plt.plot (np.arange (0.100), H.history ["val_acc"],
label = "val_acc")
```

```
8      plt.title ("Training Loss and Accuracy")

9      plt.xlabel ("Epoch #")

10     plt.ylabel ("Loss / Accuracy")

11     plt.legend ()

12     plt.show ()
```

Running the Neural Network

With the code ready, just run the command below to see our Neural Network built on top of the fully-functioning Keras library:

```
1      carlos$ python neural_network_keras.py
```

As a result, its classification_report shows that by the end of the 100 epochs, the network was able to achieve 92% accuracy, which is a good result for this type of architecture. Just as a curiosity, Convolutional Neural Networks have the potential to achieve up to 99% accuracy (!):

Many improvements can be made to the performance of our network, but you can see that even a simple architecture performs very well.

```
● ● ●                          2. python3.6
Epoch 94/100
 - 1s - loss: 0.2806 - acc: 0.9196 - val_loss: 0.2853 - val_acc: 0.9158
Epoch 95/100
 - 1s - loss: 0.2795 - acc: 0.9200 - val_loss: 0.2840 - val_acc: 0.9157
Epoch 96/100
 - 1s - loss: 0.2784 - acc: 0.9207 - val_loss: 0.2831 - val_acc: 0.9160
Epoch 97/100
 - 1s - loss: 0.2773 - acc: 0.9206 - val_loss: 0.2821 - val_acc: 0.9163
Epoch 98/100
 - 1s - loss: 0.2762 - acc: 0.9210 - val_loss: 0.2810 - val_acc: 0.9171
Epoch 99/100
 - 1s - loss: 0.2752 - acc: 0.9211 - val_loss: 0.2801 - val_acc: 0.9169
Epoch 100/100
 - 1s - loss: 0.2742 - acc: 0.9210 - val_loss: 0.2790 - val_acc: 0.9177
[INFO] avaliando a rede neural...
             precision    recall  f1-score   support

          0       0.96      0.97      0.96      1815
          1       0.95      0.96      0.96      1927
          2       0.91      0.90      0.91      1787
          3       0.90      0.90      0.90      1754
          4       0.91      0.92      0.92      1684
          5       0.89      0.86      0.88      1624
          6       0.92      0.95      0.94      1737
          7       0.93      0.94      0.93      1781
          8       0.89      0.87      0.88      1674
          9       0.90      0.89      0.90      1717

avg / total       0.92      0.92      0.92     17500
```

Looking at the chart below, notice how the curves for training and validation datasets are practically overlapping. This is an excellent indication that there were no overfitting issues during the training phase.

161

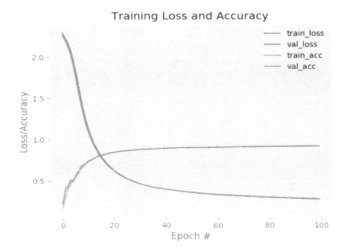

Training Loss and Accuracy

Summary of the Chapter

We have traveled these first-almost 80 years of advances in neural networks in the history of artificial intelligence. It is usually divided into three stages, from 40 to 70 where it went from the astonishment of these new models to skepticism, the return of a winter of 10 years when in the eighties there are improvements in mechanisms and ways to train the networks (backpropagation) and a plateau is reached in which the "depth" of learning cannot be reached, probably also due to lack of computing power.

And the third stage from 2006 in which this barrier is overcome and taking advantage of the power of GPUs and new ideas, it is possible to train hundreds of hierarchical layers that make up and strengthen Deep Learning, and they give an almost unlimited capacity to these networks.

Also, towards the end of the chapter, we presented the basic concepts about Neural Networks, as well as the MNIST dataset, widely used to benchmark algorithms. By testing the performance of a 4-layer neural network (input +2 hidden layers + output), we achieved 92% accuracy in the predictions made. The implementation was done on top of Keras, to show that with a few lines of code, it is possible to build great classification models.

As a last comment, I would like to say that recently (Feb 2018), there are new studies of human biological neurons in which their functioning is being rediscovered, and a new revolution is taking place since it seems that it is different from what we knew until today. This may be the beginning of a completely new and undoubtedly better stage of Deep Learning, Machine Learning, and Artificial Intelligence.

CHAPTER
EIGHT

Neural Network in Python with Keras and Tensorflow

In this chapter, we will work for creating a more advanced artificial neural network in Python with Tensorflow and Keras as the continuation of the last section of chapter 7 to learn its use in a much broader spectrum. We will implement the XOR gate and try to compare the advantages of machine learning versus traditional programming.

An Artificial Neural Network with Python and Keras

Let's see the complete code where we create a neural network with input data, the 4 combinations of XOR and its 4 ordered outputs. Then we analyze the code line by line.

```
1       import numpy as np

2       from keras.models import Sequential

3       from keras.layers.core import Dense

4

5       # we load the 4 combinations of the XOR gates
```

```
6      training_data = np.array ([[0,0], [0,1], [1,0], [1,1]],
       "float32")

7

8      # and these are the results that are obtained, in the
       same order

9      target_data = np.array ([[0], [1], [1], [0]], "float32")

10

11     model = Sequential ()

12     model.add (Dense (16, input_dim = 2, activation =
'relu'))

13     model.add (Dense (1, activation = 'sigmoid'))

14

15     model.compile (loss = 'mean_squared_error',

16             optimizer = 'adam',

17             metrics = ['binary_accuracy'])

18

19     model.fit (training_data, target_data, epochs = 1000)

20

21     # evaluate the model

22     scores = model.evaluate (training_data, target_data)

23

24     print ("\ n% s:% .2f %%"% (model.metrics_names
       [1], scores [1] * 100))

25     print (model.predict (training_data) .round ())
```

Let's Analyze the Neural Network we Made

First we import the classes we will use:

    1   import numpy as np

    2   from keras.models import Sequential

    3   from keras.layers.core import Dense

We will use numpy to handle arrays. From Keras we import the type of Sequential model and the type of Dense layer that is the "normal" one.

    1   We create the input and output arrays.

    2   # we load the 4 combinations of the XOR gates

    3   training_data = np.array ([[0,0], [0,1], [1,0], [1,1]],
            "float32")

    4

    5   # and these are the results that are obtained, in the
            same order

    6   target_data = np.array ([[0], [1], [1], [0]], "float32")

As you can see there are the four possible inputs of the XOR function [0,0], [0,1], [1,0], [1,1] and its four outputs: 0, 1,1,0.

Now we will create the architecture of our neural network:

    1   model = Sequential ()

    2   model.add (Dense (16, input_dim = 2, activation =
    'relu'))

3   model.add (Dense (1, activation = 'sigmoid'))

First, we will create an null Sequential type model. This model refers to the creation of a series of layers of sequential neurons, "one in front of the other."

We need to add two different d ense layers with the «model.add ()». It will be three layers because by putting input_dim = 2, with two neurons (for our XOR function inputs), we are defining the input layer and the first hidden (hidden) layer of 16 neurons. We will use «relu» as an active function that we know provides excellent results. It could be another function, this is a mere example, and depending on the implementation of the network we will do, we must vary the neurons number, layers, and their activation functions.

And we add a layer with one output neuron and sigmoid activation function.

Neural Network Display

Let's see what we have done so far:

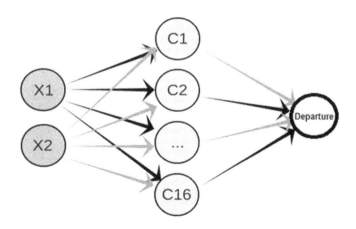

The 3-layer architecture we created for this Artificial Neural Network.

To Train the Network!

Before performing the training of the network, we will make some modifications of our model:

1   model.compile (loss = 'mean_squared_error',

2   optimizer = 'adam',

3   metrics = ['binary_accuracy'])

With this, we indicate the type of loss we will use, the "optimizer" of the weights of the neuron connections, and the metrics we want to obtain.

Now we will train the network:

1   model.fit (training_data, target_data, epochs = 1000)

We indicate with model.fit () the inputs, the outputs, and the number of training iterations (epochs) of training. This is a basic example, but keep in mind that for complex and larger models, more iterations are needed, and at the same time, the training will go slower than normal.

Training Results

If we see the training exits, we see that the first line says:

1   Epoch 1/1000

2   4/4 [=================================] -
0s 43ms / step - loss: 0.2634 - binary_accuracy:
0.5000

3   Epoch 2/1000

4   4/4 [=================================] -
0s 457us / step - loss: 0.2630 - binary_accuracy:
0.2500

With this we see that the first iteration "had some luck" and I hit half of the outputs (0.5) but from the second one, I only hit 1 in 4 (0.25).

Then in the «epoch» 24 it recovers the 0.5 of hits, it is no longer «luckily», but for having correctly adjusted the weights of the net.

1   24/1000 Epoch

2   4/4 [=================================] -
0s 482us / step - loss: 0.2549 - binary_accuracy:
0.5000

3

4   Epoch 107/1000

5   4/4 [=================================] -
0s 621us / step - loss: 0.2319 - binary_accuracy:
0.7500

6

7   Epoch 169/1000

8   4/4 [=================================] -
        0s 1ms / step - loss: 0.2142 - binary_accuracy:
        1.0000

And - in my case - in iteration 107 increases the hits to 0.75 (they are 3 out of 4) and in iteration 169 it achieves 100% hits and stays that way until it ends. Since the initial weights of the network are random, the outputs you have on your computer may be slightly different in terms of iterations, but you will reach the "binary accuracy" (binara_accuracy) of 1.0.

We Evaluate and Predict

First we evaluate the model

1   scores = model.evaluate (training_data, target_data)

2   print ("\ n% s:% .2f %%"% (model.metrics_names [1], scores [1] * 100))

And we see that we had 100% accuracy (remember the trivial of this example).

And we make the 4 possible predictions of XOR, passing our entries:

1   print (model.predict (training_data) .round ())

        and we see the 0,1,1,0 outputs that are correct.

Tuning parameters of the neural network

Remember that this is a basic example with only four possible entries. But if in reality, we had a complex network, we should be able to adjust many parameters, let's review:

- Number of layers of the network (in our case there are three)

- Number of neurons in each network (we have two input, 16 hidden layers, and one output)

- Activation functions of each layer. We use relu and sigmoid

- When compiling the model, define the functions of loss, optimizer, and metrics.

- The number of training iterations.

In this simple example, you can try to vary, for example, the numbers of input neurons - try 8 or 32 and see what results you get. For example, if you need more or fewer iterations to reach 100% of hits. We can appreciate that there are many meta-parameters to adjust. If we made the combination of all of them, we would have a terrible amount of possible adjustments. And it is above all in you, decide those parameters and adjust them.

Save the Network and Use It - Really

If this were a real case, in which we train a network, adjust it, and get good results, we should now save that network since that optimal network has the weights we were looking for. It would be silly and slow to train the network every time before "publishing in production."

What we do is save that network, and in ANOTHER code, we would load the network and use it as if it were a library or a function we created — passing tickets and getting predictions.

To save and load our network, we will use the following sample code:

```
1       # serialize the model to JSON
2       model_json = model.to_json ()
3       with open ("model.json", "w") as json_file:
4               json_file.write (model_json)
5       # serialize weights to HDF5
6       model.save_weights ("model.h5")
7       print ("Saved Model!")
8
9       # later...
10
11      # load json and create the model
12      json_file = open ('model.json', 'r')
13      loaded_model_json = json_file.read ()
14      json_file.close ()
15      loaded_model = model_from_json
(loaded_model_json)
1+6     # load weights to the new model
17      loaded_model.load_weights ("model.h5")
18      print ("Loaded model from disk.")
19
```

20   # Compile model loaded and ready to use.

21   loaded_model.compile (loss = 'mean_squared_error', optimizer = 'adam', metrics = ['binary_accuracy'])

After this, we would normally use loaded_model.predict () and voila!

Is it Worth a Neural Network? Why not Program with If-Then-Else?

After seeing all this, is it not convenient to do a "traditional" programming instead of training a neural network? Well, it will always depend on the case. For example for the XOR function we would have something like this:

```
1       function predict_XOR (input1, input2) {

2

3       if (input1 == 0 && input2 == 0) {

4               return 0;

5       } else if (entry1 == 0 && entry2 == 1) {

6               return 1;

7       } else if (entry1 == 1 && entry2 == 0) {

8               return 1;

9       } else if (entry1 == 1 && entry2 == 1) {

10              return 0;

11      }
```

```
12

13     }
```

We see that it is a function with "4 ifs" that evaluates each condition (it could be improved, I know). But what would happen if instead of 2 entries we had more parameters? ... surely the amount of "ifs" would increase creating a chaotic and error-prone code, difficult to maintain. Think about it for a moment. It does not mean that the entire code of the world must be replaced with neural networks, but it does think that in cases the neural networks give us incredible flexibility and predictive power - and that development time is justified.

Summary of the Chapter

We have created our first artificial neural network with three layers to recreate the XOR function. We have used the Keras library - and through it, Tensorflow as a backend - and we created the model, we trained the data and obtained a good result. This is the initial kick to continue seeing various architectures of Neural Networks and learn little by little with Python.

NINE

The K-Nearest-Neighbor algorithm in Python

K-Nearest-Neighbor is an instance-based algorithm of the Machine Learning supervised type. It can be used to classify new samples (discrete values) or to predict (regression, continuous values). Being a simple method, it is ideal for entering the world of Machine Learning. It essentially serves to classify values by looking for the "most similar" data points (by proximity) learned in the training stage (see seven steps to create your ML) and by guessing new points based on that classification.

Unlike K-means, which is an unsupervised algorithm and where the "K" means the amount of "groups" (clusters) that we want to classify, in K-Nearest Neighbor the "K" means the amount of "neighboring points" We take into account nearby to classify the "n" groups - which are already known in advance, as it is a supervised algorithm.

What is the k-Nearest Neighbor Algorithm?

It is a method that searches the observations closest to the one that is trying to predict and classifies the point of interest-based on the majority of data around it. As we said before, it is an algorithm:

- **Supervised:** this - briefly - means that we have labeled our training data set, with the expected class or result given "a row" of data.

- **Instance-Based:** This means that our algorithm does not explicitly learn a model (such as Logistic Regression or decision trees). Instead, it memorizes the training instances that are used as a "knowledge base" for the prediction phase.

Where does k-Nearest Neighbor Apply?

Although simple, it is used in solving many problems, such as recommendation systems, semantic search, and anomaly detection.

Pros and Cons

As a pro, it is simple to learn and implement. Its cons is that it uses the entire dataset to train "each point" and therefore requires the use of a lot of memory and processing resources (CPU). For these reasons, kNN tends to work better in small datasets and without a vast amount of features (the columns).

How does kNN Work?

1. Calculate the distance between the item to be classified and the rest of the items in the training dataset.

2. Select the nearest "k" elements (with less distance, depending on the function used)

3. Perform a "majority vote" between the k points: those of a class/label that <<domain>> will decide their final classification.

Taking into account point three, we will see that to decide the class of a point, the value of k is significant, as this will end up almost defining which group the points will belong to, especially in the "borders" between groups. For example - I would choose odd values of k to unpack beforehand (if the features we use are even). It will not be the same to take to decide three values than 13. This does not mean that necessarily taking more points implies improving accuracy. What is certain is that the more "k points," the longer our algorithm will take to process and respond.

The most popular ways of "measuring the closeness" between points are the Euclidean distance (the "usual") or the Cosine Similarity (measures the angle of the vectors, the smaller, they will be similar). Remember that this algorithm - and practically everyone in ML - works best with several features from which we take data (the columns of our dataset). What we understand as "distance" in real life will be abstract to many dimensions that we cannot easily "visualize" (such as on a map).

Let's make an Example k-Nearest Neighbor in Python

Let's explore the algorithm with Scikit learn

We will perform an exercise using Python and its scikit-learn library that has already implemented the algorithm to simplify things. Let's see how it is done.

Project Requirements

To perform this project, we will create a Jupyter notebook with Python code and the SkLearn library widely used in Data Science. We recommend using Anaconda's python suite. You can reread

177

chapter 2, where I show step by step how to install the development environment.

The Exercise and the Code: App Reviews

For our exercise, we will take 257 records with user reviews on an app (Reviews). We will use two columns of data as the food source of the algorithm. Remember that I will only take two features to be able to graph in 2 dimensions, BUT for a problem "in real life," it is better to take more features than we want to solve. This is for teaching purposes only.

The columns we will use will be wordcount with the number of words used and sentiment value with a value between -4 and 4 that indicates whether the comment was positive or negative. Our tags will be the stars that users gave to the app, which are discrete values from 1 to 5. We can think that if the user scores with more stars, they will have a positive feeling, but it is not necessarily always the case.

Let's Start with the Code!

First, we make imports of libraries that we will use for data management, graphics, and our algorithm.

```
1    import pandas as pd

2    import numpy as np

3    import matplotlib.pyplot as plt

4    from matplotlib.colors import ListedColormap

5    import matplotlib.patches as mpatches
```

```
6      import seaborn as sb

7

8      % matplotlib inline

9      plt.rcParams ['figure.figsize'] = (16, 9)

10     plt.style.use ('ggplot')

11

12     from sklearn.model_selection import train_test_split

13     from sklearn.preprocessing import MinMaxScaler

14     from sklearn.neighbors import KNeighborsClassifier

15     from sklearn.metrics import classification_report

16     from sklearn.metrics import confusion_matrix
```

We load the CSV input file with pandas, using a semicolon separator because, in the reviews, there are texts that use a comma. With head (10), we see the first ten records.

We take the opportunity to see a statistical summary of the data:

	wordcount	Star Rating	sentimentValue
count	257.000000	257.000000	257.000000
mean	11.501946	3.420233	0.383849
std	13.159812	1.409531	0.897987
min	1.000000	1.000000	-2.276469
25%	3.000000	3.000000	-0.108144
50%	7.000000	3.000000	0.264091
75%	16.000000	5.000000	0.808384
max	103.000000	5.000000	3.264579

There are 257 records. The stars logically see that they go from 1 to 5. The number of words goes from 1 only to 103. And the feeling ratings are between -2.27 and 3.26 with an average of 0.38, and from the standard deviation, we can see that most they are between 0.38-0.89 and 0.38 + 0.89.

A Bit of Visualization

Let's see some simple graphs and what information they give us:

1   dataframe.hist ()

2   plt.show ()

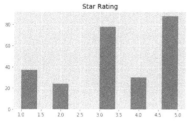

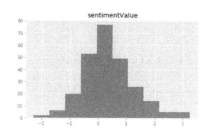

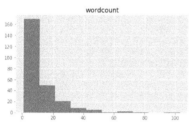

We see that the distribution of "stars" is not balanced ... this is not good. It would be convenient to have the same quantities at the outputs, so as not to have "biased" results. For this exercise, we will leave it that way, but in real life, we must balance them. The Sentiment Values graph looks quite like a bell moved slightly to the right of zero, and the number of words is centered mostly from 0 to 10.

Let's see how many Star Ratings we have:

```
1       print (dataframe.groupby ('Star Rating'). size ())
```

```
Star Rating
1    37
2    24
3    78
4    30
5    88
dtype: int64
```

With that, we confirm that there are mostly 3 and 5 stars.

We Prepare the Tickets

We create our X and Y input and training and test sets.

```
1    X = dataframe [['wordcount', 'sentimentValue']].
Values

2    y = dataframe ['Star Rating']. values

3

4    X_train, X_test, y_train, y_test = train_test_split (X,
     y, random_state = 0)

5    scaler = MinMaxScaler ()

6    X_train = scaler.fit_transform (X_train)

7    X_test = scaler.transform (X_test)
```

Let's use k-Nearest Neighbor with Scikit Learn

We define the value of k in 7 (we really know this later, you'll see) and create our classifier.

```
1    n_neighbors = 7

2

3    knn = KNeighborsClassifier (n_neighbors)

4    knn.fit (X_train, y_train)

5    print ('Accuracy of K-NN classifier on training set:
     {: .2f}'
```

```
6    .          format (knn.score (X_train, y_train)))

7        print ('Accuracy of K-NN classifier on test set: {:
.2f}'

8    .          format (knn.score (X_test, y_test)))
```

Accuracy of K-

NN classifier on test set: 0.86

We see that the accuracy it gives us is 90% in the training set and 86% for the test set.

NOTE: As you will see, we use the SciKit Learn KNeighborsClassifier class since our labels are discrete values (stars 1 to 5). But you should know that there is also the KneighborsRegressor class for labels with continuous values.

Model Accuracy

Let's confirm the accuracy by looking at the Matrix Confusion and the Report on the test set, which details the successes and failures:

```
1      pred = knn.predict (X_test)

2      print (confusion_matrix (y_test, pred))

3      print (classification_report (y_test, pred))
```

```
[[ 9  0  1  0  0]
 [ 0  1  0  0  0]
 [ 0  1 17  0  1]
 [ 0  0  2  8  0]
 [ 0  0  4  0 21]]
              precision    recall  f1-score   support

           1       1.00      0.90      0.95        10
           2       0.50      1.00      0.67         1
           3       0.71      0.89      0.79        19
           4       1.00      0.80      0.89        10
           5       0.95      0.84      0.89        25

avg / total        0.89      0.86      0.87        65
```

How the F1 score looks is 87%, quite good.

NOTE: Remember that this is just an exercise to learn, and we have VERY few total records and in our test set. For example, two stars have only 1 rating, and this is insufficient.

And now, the Graphic we wanted to See!

Now we will make the graph with the classification obtained, which helps us to easily see where the predictions will fall. NOTE: being 2 features, we can make the 2D graph and if they were 3 it could be in 3D. But for real uses, we could have more than 3 dimensions and it would not matter to be able to visualize it but the result of the algorithm.

1   h = .02 # step size in the mesh

2

3   # Create color maps

4   cmap_light = ListedColormap (['# FFAAAA', '# ffcc99', '# ffffb3', '# b3ffff', '# c2f0c2'])

```
5    cmap_bold = ListedColormap (['# FF0000', '# ff9933', '#
     FFFF00', '# 00ffff', '# 00FF00'])

6

7    # we create an instance of Neighbors Classifier and fit the
     data.

8    clf = KNeighborsClassifier (n_neighbors, weights =
     'distance')

9    clf.fit (X, y)

10

11   # Plot the decision boundary. For that, we will assign a
     color to each

12   # point in the mesh [x_min, x_max] x [y_min, y_max].

13   x_min, x_max = X [:, 0] .min () - 1, X [:, 0] .max () + 1

14   y_min, y_max = X [:, 1] .min () - 1, X [:, 1] .max () + 1

15   xx, yy = np.meshgrid (np.arange (x_min, x_max, h),

16              np.arange (y_min, y_max, h))

17   Z = clf.predict (np.c_ [xx.ravel (), yy.ravel ()])

18

19   # Put the result into a color plot

20   Z = Z.reshape (xx.shape)

21   plt.figure ()

22   plt.pcolormesh (xx, yy, Z, cmap = cmap_light)
```

23

254 # Plot also the training points

25 plt.scatter (X [:, 0], X [:, 1], c = y, cmap = cmap_bold,

26   edgecolor = 'k', s = 20)

27 plt.xlim (xx.min (), xx.max ())

28 plt.ylim (yy.min (), yy.max ())

29

30 patch0 = mpatches.Patch (color = '# FF0000', label = '1')

31 patch1 = mpatches.Patch (color = '# ff9933', label = '2')

32 patch2 = mpatches.Patch (color = '# FFFF00', label = '3')

33 patch3 = mpatches.Patch (color = '# 00ffff', label = '4')

34 patch4 = mpatches.Patch (color = '# 00FF00', label = '5')

35 plt.legend (handles = [patch0, patch1, patch2, patch3, patch4])

36

37

38 plt.title ("5-Class classification (k =% i, weights = '% s')"

39   % (n_neighbors, weights))

40

41 plt.show ()

We see the 5 areas in which the number of words is related to the feeling value of the Review that the user leaves.

The 5 regions could be divided as follows:

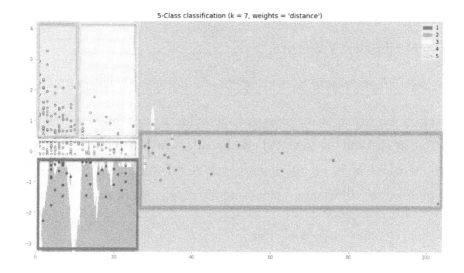

That is to say that "by eye," a review of 20 words and Sentiment 1, would give us an assessment of 4 (celestial zone).

With these areas, we can intuit specific characteristics of the users who use and value the app:

- Users who put 1 star have negative feelings and up to 25 words.

- Users who put two stars give many explanations (up to 100 words), and their feeling can vary between negative and something positive.

- Users who put three stars are quite neutral in feelings since they are around zero and up to about 25 words.

- Users who give five stars are quite positive (from 0.5 onwards, approximately) and put a few words (up to 10).

Choose the Best Value of k

(Especially important for unpacking or choosing border points!)

Before we saw that we assigned the value n_neighbors = 7 as the value of «k» and we obtained good results. But where did that value come from? Well, I really had to execute this code that comes next, where we see different k values and the precision obtained.

```
1    k_range = range (1, 20)

2    scores = []

3    for k in k_range:

4            knn = KNeighborsClassifier (n_neighbors = k)

5            knn.fit (X_train, y_train)

6            scores.append (knn.score (X_test, y_test))

7    plt.figure ()

8    plt.xlabel ('k')

9    plt.ylabel ('accuracy')

10   plt.scatter (k_range, scores)

11   plt.xticks ([0,5,10,15,20])
```

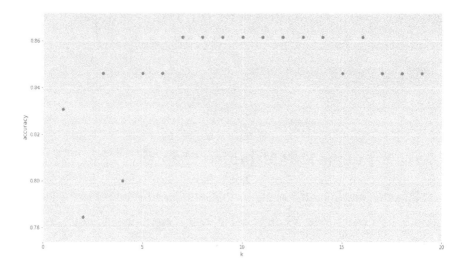

In the graph we see that with values k = 7 ak = 14 is where greater precision is achieved.

Classify and/or Predict New Samples

We already have our model and our value of k. Now, the logical thing will be to use it! Well, suppose we get new reviews! Let's see how to predict your stars in two ways. The first:

1   print (clf.predict ([[5, 1.0]]))

        [5]

This result indicates that for five words and feel one, we will rate the app with five stars.

But we could also obtain the probabilities that give us 1, 2,3,4 or 5 stars with predict_proba ():

1   print (clf.predict_proba ([[20, 0.0]]))

        [[0.00381998 0.02520212 0.97097789 0. 0.]]

189

Here we see that for coordinates 20, 0.0, 97% we have a probability of three stars. You can check in the previous graph that they fit in the areas that we delimited above.

Summary of the kNN Algorithm Chapter

In this exercise, we created a Python model to process and classify points of an input set with the k-Nearest Neighbor algorithm. As its name says, the "k closest neighbors" are evaluated to classify new points. Being a supervised algorithm, we must have enough labeled samples to be able to train the model with good results.

This algorithm is quite simple, and, as we saw before, we need many memory and CPU resources to keep the dataset "alive" and evaluate new points. This does not make it advisable for vast data sets. In the example, we only use two input dimensions to be able to graph and see in two dimensions how the groups are obtained and delimited. Finally, we were able to make new predictions and following the results.

CHAPTER
TEN

Weather Series Forecast Exercise with Neural Networks in Python

In this final chapter, we will see what time series are and how to predict their behavior using neural networks with Keras and Tensorflow. We will review the complete code in Python with the proposed exercise with the input data.

What is a Time Series and Why is it Special?

A time series is a set of samples taken at regular time intervals. It is interesting to analyze their behavior in the medium and long term, trying to detect patterns and be able to forecast how their future behavior will be. What makes a Time Series << special >> unlike a Regression «problem» are two things:

- It is time-dependent. This breaks the requirement that linear regression has for its observations to be independent.

- They usually have some type of seasonality, or trends to grow or decrease. Consider how much more product sells an ice cream shop in just 4 months a year than in the other seasons.

Example Time Series Are:

- Capture the temperature, humidity, and pressure of an area at 15-minute intervals.

- Value of the shares of a company in the stock market minute by minute.

- Daily (or monthly) sales of a company.

- Production in kg of a harvest every semester.

I think that with that they already have an idea. As you can also see, the time series can be 1 variable or multiple.

We will start with the practice, loading a dataset that contains information on almost 2 years of daily sales of products. The fields it contains are date and the number of units sold.

Requirements for the Exercise

As always, to be able to carry out the practices, I recommend that you have a Python 3.6 environment installed, such as Anaconda, which already provides us with the Jupyter Notebooks, as explained in this chapter. It can also be run on the command line without problems. This exercise also requires having Keras and Tensorflow (or other similar) installed, as explained in the previous chapters.

Load the Example with Pandas Library

We will take advantage of the benefits of Pandas to load and process our data. We start by importing the libraries we will use and reading the csv file.

```
1    import pandas as pd

2    import numpy as np

3    import matplotlib.pylab as plt

4    % matplotlib inline

5    plt.rcParams ['figure.figsize'] = (16, 9)

6    plt.style.use ('fast')

7

8    from keras.models import Sequential

9    from keras.layers import Dense, Activation, Flatten

10   from sklearn.preprocessing import MinMaxScaler

11

12   df = pd.read_csv ('time_series.csv', parse_dates = [0], header
     = None, index_col = 0, squeeze = True, names = ['date',
     'units'])

13   df.head ()

     Date
```

2017-01-02 236

2017-01-03 237

2017-01-04 290

2017-01-05 221

2017-01-07 128

Name: units, dtype: int64

Let's notice one thing before continuing: the dataframe that we carry with pandas has as an index our first column with dates . This is to allow us to filter by date directly and some special operations.

For example, we can see what dates we have data with:

```
1    print (df.index.min ())
2    print (df.index.max ())
     2017-01-02 00:00:00
     2018-11-30 00:00:00
```

Presumably, we have daily sales of 2017 and 2018 until November. And now let's see how many samples we have each year:

```
1    print (len (df ['2017']))
2    print (len (df ['2018']))
     315
     289
```

As this trade closes on Sundays, we see that in 2017, we do not have 365 days as we could erroneously assume. And in 2018 we have the last month ... which will be what we will try to predict.

Data Display

Let's see some graphs about the data we have. But first ... let's take advantage of the statistical data that pandas give us with describe ()

1   df.describe ()

count 604.000000

mean 215.935430

std 75.050304

min 51.000000

25% 171.000000

50% 214.000000

75% 261.250000

max 591.000000

Name: units, dtype: float64

There are a total of 604 records, the average sales of units are 215 and a deviation of 75, that is to say, that we will usually be between 140 and 290 units.

In fact, let's take advantage of having an index of dates with pandas and take out the monthly averages:

```
1    months = df.resample ('M'). mean ()

2    months
```

Date

2017-01-31 203.923077

2017-02-28 184.666667

2017-03-31 182.964286

2017-04-30 198.960000

2017-05-31 201.185185

2017-06-30 209.518519

2017-07-31 278.923077

2017-08-31 316.000000

2017 -09-30 222.925926

2017-10-31 207.851852

2017-11-30 185.925926

2017-12-31 213.200000

2018-01-31 201.384615

2018-02-28 190.625000

2018-03-31 174.846154

2018-04-30 186.000000

2018-05 -31 190.666667

2018-06-30 196.037037

2018-07-31 289.500000

2018-08-31 309.038462

2018-09-30 230.518519

2018-10-31 209.444444

2018-11-30 184.481481

Freq: M, Name: units, dtype: float64

And let's visualize those monthly averages:

1   plt.plot (months ['2017']. values)

2   plt.plot (months ['2018']. values)

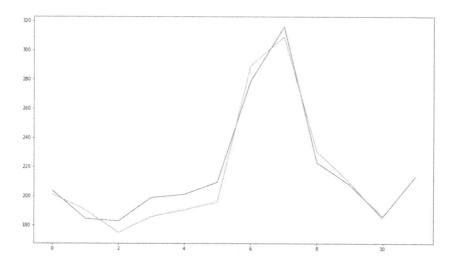

We see that in 2017 (in blue) we have a beginning of the year with a decrease in the number of units, then it begins to rise until the arrival of the European summer where in June and July we have the largest amount of sales. Finally decreases again and has a small peak in December with Christmas.

We also see that 2018 (orange) behaves practically the same. In other words, it seems that we have a seasonality. For example, we could venture to predict that «the summer of 2019 will also have a peak in sales».

Let's see the chart of daily sales (in units) in June and July

```
1      summer2017 = df ['2017-06-01': '2017-09-01']

2      plt.plot (summer2017.values)

3      summer2018 = df ['2018-06-01': '2018-09-01']

4      plt.plot (summer2018.values)
```

How to Forecast Time Series

Once we have confirmed that our series is stationary, we can forecast. There are various methods for forecasting. In our case, sales seem to behave quite similar to the year, with which a simple method if for example, we wanted to provide the stock that this trade would need, would be to say «If in 2017 in December we sold an average of 213 units, I predict that in December it will be similar».

Well, we who are such advanced and applied students will use Machine Learning: a neural network to make the forecast. Curiously, creating this network is relatively simple, and in a short time, we will be using a modern model to make the forecast.

Daily Sales Forecast with Neural Networks

We will use a simple architecture of the FeedForward neural network (also called MLP by its acronym Multi-Layered Perceptron), with few neurons and as a method of hyperbolic tangent activation as we will deliver transformed values between -1 and 1.

Prepare the Data

This may be one of the most important steps in this exercise.

What we will do is alter our input stream of the csv file that contains a column with the dispatched units, and we will convert it into several columns. And why do this?

Actually, what we will do is take our time series and turn it into a "supervised type problem" to feed our neural network and be able to train it with backpropagation ("as usual"). To do this, we must have some inputs and outputs to train the model.

What we will do - in this example - is to take the previous 7 days to "get" the eighth. We could try to train the network with 2 or 3 days. Or we could have only 1 way out, or even "dare" try to predict more than one "future day." I leave that to you as an extra activity. But then let's stay with that:

- **Tickets:** will be "7 columns" representing sales in units of the previous 7 days.

- **Departure:** The value of the «8th day». That is the sales (in pcs) of that day.

To make this transformation, I will use a function called series_to_supervised (). (You will see it in the code, below)

Before using the function, we use the MinMaxScaler to transform the range of our values between -1 and 1 (since we know that our neural network favors you to perform the calculations).

So here we see how our set of input data looks.

```
1     STEPS = 7

2

3     # convert series to supervised learning

4     def series_to_supervised (data, n_in = 1, n_out = 1, dropnan = True):

5             n_vars = 1 if type (data) is list else data.shape [1]

6             df = pd.DataFrame (data)

7             cols, names = list (), list ()

8             # input sequence (t-n, ... t-1)

9             for i in range (n_in, 0, -1):

10                    cols.append (df.shift (i))

11                    names += = [('var% d (t-% d)'% (j + 1, i)) for j in range (n_vars)]

12            # forecast sequence (t, t + 1, ... t + n)
```

```
13          for i in range (0, n_out):
14                  cols.append (df.shift (-i))
15                      if i == 0:
16          names + = [('var% d (t)'% (j + 1)) for j in range
            (n_vars)]
17                      else:
18          names + = [('var% d (t +% d)'% (j + 1, i)) for j in
            range (n_vars)]
19          # put it all together
20          agg = pd.concat (cols, axis = 1)
21          agg.columns = names
22          # drop rows with NaN values
23          if dropnan:
24                  agg.dropna (inplace = True)
25          return agg
26
27          # load dataset
28          values = df.values
29          # ensure all data is float
30          values = values.astype ('float32')
31          # normalize features
```

```
32          scaler = MinMaxScaler (feature_range = (- 1, 1))

33      values = values.reshape (-1, 1) # this we do because we
        have 1 single dimension

34              scaled = scaler.fit_transform (values)

35              # frame as supervised learning

36              reframed = series_to_supervised (scaled, STEPS, 1)

37              reframed.head ()
```

	var1(t-7)	var1(t-6)	var1(t-5)	var1(t-4)	var1(t-3)	var1(t-2)	var1(t-1)	var1(t)
7	-0.314815	-0.311111	-0.114815	-0.370370	-0.714815	-0.103704	-0.225926	-0.433333
8	-0.311111	-0.114815	-0.370370	-0.714815	-0.103704	-0.225926	-0.433333	-0.607407
9	-0.114815	-0.370370	-0.714815	-0.103704	-0.225926	-0.433333	-0.607407	-0.522222
10	-0.370370	-0.714815	-0.103704	-0.225926	-0.433333	-0.607407	-0.522222	-0.644444
11	-0.714815	-0.103704	-0.225926	-0.433333	-0.607407	-0.522222	-0.644444	-0.344444

We will use as columns the columns headed as var1 (t-7) to (t-1), and our output (what would be the "Y" value of the function) will be var1 (t) -the last column-.

We Create the Artificial Neural Network

Before creating the neural network, we will subdivide our data set into train and validation. ATTENTION, something important in this procedure, unlike in other problems in which we can "mix" the input data, is that in this case, we care to maintain the order in which we will feed the network.

Therefore, we will make a subdivision of the first 567 consecutive days for network training and the next 30 for validation. This is a proportion that I chose, and that I found convenient, but definitely, it may not be the optimum (it is proposed to the reader, vary this proportion for example to 80-20 and compare results)

```
1      # split into train and test sets

2      values = reframed.values

3      n_train_days = 315 + 289 - (30 + STEPS)

4      train = values [: n_train_days,:]

5      test = values [n_train_days :,:]

6      # split into input and outputs

7      x_train, y_train = train [:,: -1], train [:, -1]

8      x_val, y_val = test [:,: -1], test [:, -1]

9      # reshape input to be 3D [samples, timesteps, features]

10     x_train = x_train.reshape ((x_train.shape [0], 1, x_train.shape
       [1]))

11     x_val = x_val.reshape ((x_val.shape [0], 1, x_val.shape [1]))

12     print (x_train.shape, y_train.shape, x_val.shape, y_val.shape)

       (567, 1, 7) (567,) (30, 1, 7) (30,)
```

We have transformed the entry into an array with form (567,1,7). This to means something like "567 entries with 1 × 7 vectors".

The architecture of the neural network will be:

- Input 7 inputs, as we said before

- 1 hidden layer with 7 neurons (I chose this value, but it can be varied)

- The output will be 1 single neuron

- As an activation function, we use hyperbolic tangent since we will use values between -1 and 1.

- We will use Adam as an optimizer and loss metric Mean Absolute Error

- As the prediction will be a continuous and non-discrete value, to calculate the Acuracy we will use Mean Squared Error and to know if it improves with the training it should be reduced with the EPOCHS.

```
1    def create_modeloFF ():
2            model = Sequential ()
3    model.add (Dense (STEPS, input_shape = (1, STEPS),
     activation = 'tanh'))
4            model.add (Flatten ())
5            model.add (Dense (1, activation = 'tanh'))
6    model.compile (loss = 'mean_absolute_error', optimizer =
     'Adam', metrics = ["mse"])
7            model.summary ()
8            return model
9
```

Training and Results

Let's see how our machine behaves after 40 times.

```
1       EPOCHS = 40

2

3       model = create_modeloFF ()

4

5       history = model.fit (x_train, y_train, epochs = EPOCHS,
        validation_data = (x_val, y_val), batch_size = STEPS)
```

In a few seconds we see a reduction in the loss value of both the training set and the validation set.

Epoch 40/40

567/567 [================================] - 0s 554us / step - loss: 0.1692 - mean_squared_error : 0.0551 - val_loss: 0.1383 - val_mean_squared_error: 0.03

We visualize the validation set (remember that it was 30 days)

```
1       results = model.predict (x_val)

2       plt.scatter (range (len (y_val)), y_val, c = 'g')

3       plt.scatter (range (len (results)), results, c = 'r')

4       plt.title ('validate')

5       plt.show ()
```

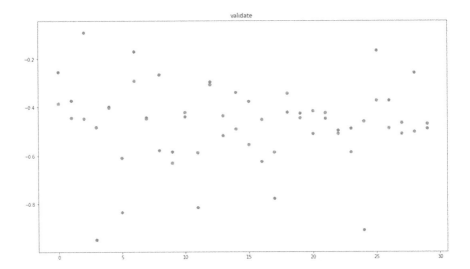

validate

In the graph we see that the green dots try to approach the red ones. The closer or overlap the better. TIP: If we increase the number of EPOCHS it improves more and more.

Forecast of Future Sales

Now that we have our network and - assuming that we perform the 7 steps of the ML - we take it for good; we will try to make a new prediction, in this case, we will use the last days of November 2018 to calculate the first week of December. Let's see:

1   Last Days = df ['2018-11-16': '2018-11-30']

2   last days

       Date

       2018-11-16 152

       2018-11-17 111

       2018-11-19 207

2018-11-20 206

2018-11-21 183

2018-11-22 200

2018-11-23 187

2018-11-24 189

2018 -11-25 76

2018-11-26 276

2018-11-27 220

2018-11-28 183

2018-11-29 251

2018-11-30 189

Name: units, dtype: int64

And now, we will follow the same data preprocessing we did for the training: scaling the values, calling the function series_to_supervised, but this time without including the output column "Y" because it is the one we want to find. Therefore, you will see in the code that we do drop () of the last column.

1   values = last Days.values

2   values = values.astype ('float32')

3   # normalize features

4   values = values.reshape (-1, 1) # this we do because we have 1 single dimension

5   scaled = scaler.fit_transform (values)

6   reframed = series_to_supervised (scaled, STEPS, 1)

7   reframed.drop (reframed.columns [[7]], axis = 1, inplace = True)

8   reframed.head (7)

	var1(t-7)	var1(t-6)	var1(t-5)	var1(t-4)	var1(t-3)	var1(t-2)	var1(t-1)
7	-0.24	-0.65	0.31	0.30	0.07	0.24	0.11
8	-0.65	0.31	0.30	0.07	0.24	0.11	0.13
9	0.31	0.30	0.07	0.24	0.11	0.13	-1.00
10	0.30	0.07	0.24	0.11	0.13	-1.00	1.00
11	0.07	0.24	0.11	0.13	-1.00	1.00	0.44
12	0.24	0.11	0.13	-1.00	1.00	0.44	0.07
13	0.11	0.13	-1.00	1.00	0.44	0.07	0.75

From this set "last days" we take only the last row, as it corresponds to the last week of November and leaves it in the correct format for the neural network with reshape:

1   values = reframed.values

2   x_test = values [6 :,:]

3   x_test = x_test.reshape ((x_test.shape [0], 1, x_test.shape [1]))

4   x_test

array ([[[0.11000001, 0.13, -1., 1.,

0.44000006, 0.06999993, 0.75]]], dtype = float32)

Now we will create a function to "fill in" the displacement we make for each prediction. This is because we want to predict the first 7 days of December. So by December 1, we already have the set with the last 7 days of November.

But to forecast December 2 we need the previous 7 days that INCLUDE December 1 and that value, we get it in our previous prediction. And so on until December 7.

```
1    def addNewValue (x_test, newValue):
2         for i in range (x_test.shape [2] -1):
3              x_test [0] [0] [i] = x_test [0] [0] [i + 1]
4              x_test [0] [0] [x_test.shape [2] -1] = new Value
5         return x_test
6
7    results = []
8    for i in range (7):
9         partial = model.predict (x_test)
10        results.append (partial [0])
11        print (x_test)
12        x_test = addNewValue (x_test, partial [0])
```

We almost have it… Now the predictions are in the domain of -1 to 1 and we want it in our "real" scale of units sold. Then we will "re-transform" the data with the "scaler" object we created before.

```
1    adimen = [x for x in results]

2    inverted = scaler.inverse_transform (adimen)

3    inverted
```

array ([[174.48904094],

[141.26934129],

[225.49292353],

[203.73262324],

[177.30941712],

[208.1552254],

[175.23698644]])

We can now create a new DataFrame Pandas in case we want to save a new csv with the forecast. And we visualize it.

```
1    prediccion1WeekDecember = pda DataFrame (inverted)

2    prediccion1SemanaDiciembre.columns = ['forecast']

3    prediccion1WeekDecember.plot ()

4    prediccion1SemanaDiciembre.to_csv ('pronostico.csv')
```

From the last 7 days of November 2018 and using our neural network, we made the following forecast of unit sales for the first week of December.

Conclusions and Proposal to the Reader

During this final chapter of machine learning, we differentiate what the Time Series are and their prediction of Regression problems. We take advantage of the ability of neural networks to generalize and predict future sales.

One of the most important steps, when pre-processing, is to convert our series into a supervised learning model, where we have input and output values, to train the network. And we end up making a week forecast using the neural network created.

I propose to the reader to make several tests to improve the predictions, altering exercise parameters:

- Vary the amount of EPOCHS

- Try another optimizer other than Adam, or set values other than Learning Rate.

- Change the architecture of the Neural Network:

   o Change the number of Neurons in the hidden layer.

   o Add more hidden layers

- Test using more than 7 days before to predict. Or try with fewer days.

- You can try trying to predict more than 1 day at a time (without iterating the result as I did with the function AddNewValue ())

NOTE: Remember that the future is UNPREDICTABLE ... so I must tell the Data Scientist: be careful, especially if we must predict results of a series with erratic behavior, such as stock market values! And also use caution in sensitive matters related to topics such as health.

Conclusion

Hardly any other field of research has attracted so much attention lately as machine learning (ML) with the associated rapid advances in the field of artificial intelligence (AI).

Recent achievements in the field of machine-long learning (ML) have an enormous contribution to the further development of artificial intelligence (AI) and made cognitive systems. AI has become a global economic and strategic, highly relevant factor. In the future, people will encounter in many contexts learning systems.

There is hardly an area that is transformed not based AI of ML and mature technologies, be it the production of goods in the context of industry 4.0, healthcare with AI assistant for better diagnostics, our mobility with autonomous vehicles or a clean and safe energy supply where intelligent computer programs ensure optimal control. But our education and work are increasingly influenced by intelligent systems that can help us and learn from us.

In the future, machines will increasingly generate decision-relevant results. For this, it is crucial to ensure making processes on the technological side of the security, robustness, and adequate traceability of automated decisions.

At the same time must be ensured is that ML applications compatible with legal issues such as liability and responsibility for decisions made algorithmically and technically environmentally settable. This regulative to formulate and implement is an important and complex issue that requires an inter and trans-disciplinary approach.

Machine Learning Applications

To review the different applications of ML, we will first differentiate between Supervised and Unsupervised Learning and Reinforcement Learning once again.

Supervised Learning

In Supervised Learning, the data for training includes the desired solution, called "labels." A clear example is when classifying incoming mail between spam or not. Among the various features that we want to train, we must include whether it is junk mail or not with a 1 or a 0.

Another example is when predicting numerical values , for example, housing price from its characteristics (square meters, number of rooms, includes heating, distance from the center, etc.), and we must include the price we find in our data set.

The most used algorithms in Supervised Learning are:

- k-Nearest Neighbors
- Linear Regression
- Logistic Regression
- Support Vector Machines
- Bayesian Classifiers

- Decision Trees and Random Forest

- Neural Networks

- Deep learning

Unsupervised Learning

Non-Supervised learning training data does not include Labels, and the algorithm will attempt to classify or decrypt the information by itself. An example in which it is used is to group the information collected about users on a Web or in an app and that our Intelligence detects various characteristics that they have in common.

The most important algorithms of Unsupervised Learning are:

- K-Means Clustering

- Principal Component Analysis

- Anomaly Detection

Reinforcement Learning

Our system will be an "autonomous agent" who must explore an unknown "space" and determine the actions to be carried out by trial and error. You will learn for yourself by obtaining prizes -rewards- and penalties the optimal way to travel a path, solve a puzzle, or behave, for example, in the Pac Man or the Flappy Bird. It will create the best possible strategy (policies) to obtain the highest potential reward promptly. Policies will define what actions to take in each situation you face.

- Markov Decision Processes (MDP: Markov Decision Process)

ML Applications and Examples

The most frequent applications of Machine Learning are:

Image Recognition

Various algorithms are used to understand images, especially Deep Learning), find something in particular or group zones. We know that the images are sets of continuous pixels, and each one contains information about the color that has to be "illuminated" (for example, RGB).

Typical examples are OCR Optical Character Recognition, that is, finding letters, grouping them, finding spaces and being able to decipher texts and the other example is to detect people in images, human presence in security cameras or more recently networks are used convolutional neuronal to detect faces: facial recognition, surely more than once Facebook was able to locate your cousins and brothers in your photo albums.

Speech Recognition

From the sound waves synthesized by the microphone of your computer, smartphone or your car, Machine Learning algorithms are able to clean noise, intuit the silences between words and understand your language to interpret your orders, whether «Siri, Add a Reminder for next Monday »or« Ok Google, Play Coldplay music »or even make reservations and order pizza. Part of the recognition is done through Natural Language Processing (NLP).

Classification

It consists of identifying to which Class each individual of the population we are analyzing belongs. You will be assigned a discrete value of type 1, 0, as in the spam classification or not. It could also be to classify whether a tumor is benign or not or when classifying flowers according to the characteristics obtained.

Prediction

Similar to the classification, but for continuous values, it allows us to try to predict what value we will obtain, given a set of input data with an unknown result. As we mentioned before, it can be used to predict prices of real estate, rentals, cars, or the probability of an event frequently used in statistics with Linear Regression. But if what we want to do is Time Series Forecast, it will be better to use neural networks or other statistical models such as ARIMA.

Hearing Segmentation

Unsupervised learning is often used to create and discover unfamiliar patterns in the behavior of customers of a website, app, or business. These algorithms can discover groups that we did not entirely know or group specific characteristics that correlate and that we would hardly have identified.

Games

We can use ML to give intelligence to the enemies that the user (protagonist) of the game has to face. It is also used to make our troops know how to move and jump obstacles on a battlefield.

Autonomous Car

In this field, many of the investigations in Machine Learning are being carried out to give cars a life of their own. One of the uses will be for the car to move the steering wheel by itself, analyzing the images, also to detect other vehicles and not to crash and even predict how others are moving to avoid accidents. Detect symbols of speed, Stop, school zone on the road. The car has many decisions to make and in a very short time, being all crucial and high priority. It is a fascinating case study for Machine Learning and is becoming a reality.

Health

Given the symptoms presented by a patient in an anonymous patient database, our machine should be able to predict whether it is likely that this person could suffer a specific disease. This type of Machine Learning is very delicate and can serve as support for a medical team.

Economy and Finance

Financial analysts can be supported trying to predict specific stock quotes on the Exchange, helping to decide whether to buy, hold, or sell.

Recommendation Engines

We watch a movie or a series. Millions of people watch that same series. Wouldn't it be logical that I like another movie that other users saw with a profile similar to mine? Well, that's what Netflix and other providers take advantage of to be able to recommend content to their users. Amazon is famous for its "If you carry that product, you will also be interested in this one." This is also achieved with this type of Machine Learning Applications.

Machine learning and artificial intelligence have become an economically, socially, and strategically high relevant topic. Their use in more and more applications competition is crucial. In particular, the US and China are among the strongest competitors. Thus, back issues to research and development, adequate staff, available data, and commercial applications increasingly becoming the focus of politics, science, and other industries globally.

References

https://www.kaggle.com/

https://plot.ly/

https://towardsdatascience.com/

https://data-science-blog.com/

https://machinelearningblogs.com/

https://mikekling.com/analyzing-the-billboard-hot-100/

https://www.datasciencecentral.com/profiles/blogs/deep-learning-an-overview

https://developer.ibm.com/articles/ cc-beginner-guide-machine-learning-ai-cognitive/

https://broutonlab.com/blog/tutotial-create-simple-neural-netowrk

http://scikit-learn.org/stable/auto_examples/neighbors/plot_classification.html

https://pythonspot.com/category/machine-learning/

https://pythonspot.com/tag/machine-learning/

https://scipy-lectures.org/packages/scikit-learn/auto_examples/plot_iris_knn.html

https://www.cs.colostate.edu/~cs545/fall16/doku.php?id=code:nearest_neighbors

https://towardsdatascience.com/solving-a-simple-classification-problem-with-python-fruits-lovers-edition-d20ab6b071d2

https://datascienceplus.com/machine-learning-for-diabetes-with-python/

https://gist.github.com/ChrisDeSantis/e24508b3c55fe536c35f6cdbf3787b68

https://github.com/prakatheesh1234/Machine-learning-code-for-Diabetes/blob/master/main

https://gist.github.com/anandology/772d44d291a9daa198d4

http://scikit-learn.org/stable/auto_examples/classification/plot_classifier_comparison.html

https://pythonspot.com/category/pro/tutorials/

http://keras.io/getting-started/sequential-model-guide/

https://github.com/glouppe/tutorials-scikit-learn/blob/master/robustness.py

https://www.bogotobogo.com/python/files/NeuralNetworks/nn3.py

https://github.com/zhuang-li/SparkNerualNetwork/blob/master/NerualNetwork.py

https://github.com/maheshakya/Time-Series-Forcasting-with-Neural-Networks/ blob/master/NeuralNet.py

https://codereview.stackexchange.com/questions/127449/ checking-convergence-of-2-layer-neural-network-in-python

https://rolisz.ro/2013/04/18/neural-networks-in-python/

https://towardsdatascience.com/ back-propagation-the-easy-way-part-2-bea37046c897

https://stackoverflow.com/questions/34098558/ gradient-descent-ann-what-is-matlab-doing-that-im-not

https://gist.github.com/ZSalloum/54703842f8a06e38fd76934579a6 c814

https://pastebin.com/w6pN5qh3

https://stackoverflow.com/questions/36014122/ neural-networks-value-errors-shapes-not-alligned

https://www.promezio.it/2017/02/26/ machine-learning-rete-neurale-minimale-xor/

https://github.com/navneetagarwal/Malicious-URL-Detection/blob/master/ Perceptron.py

https://www.labri.fr/perso/nrougier/downloads/mlp.py

www.ingramcontent.com/pod-product-compliance
Lightning Source LLC
Chambersburg PA
CBHW051049050326
40690CB00006B/661